MESOPO-
TAMIA

ASIA

INDIA

RIA

Niniue 171.

Rages 349.

Haran 110.

Persepolis

a70.

CHALDEA

Babylon 150.

Susa 230.

Damascus 40,

Vr 156.

ARABIA

Saba 512.

Das Rote Meer.

roe 24.

renland

JERUSALEM

IN THE SHADOW OF HEAVEN

DIRECTED AND EDITED BY
DAVID COHEN AND LEE LIBERMAN

TEXT BY
SUSAN WELS

DESIGNED BY
TOM MORGAN

DIRECTOR OF PHOTOGRAPHY
PETER HOWE

PHOTOGRAPHED BY MORE THAN 50 OF THE WORLD'S FOREMOST PHOTOJOURNALISTS

This book was made possible through the generous assistance of:
THE ASSOCIATION FOR PROMOTING TOURISM IN ISRAEL
EASTMAN KODAK COMPANY
HOLIDAY INN CROWNE PLAZA JERUSALEM
AFRICA ISRAEL HOTELS & RESORTS LTD.
KESHER RENT A CAR LTD/HERTZ LICENSEE

CollinsPublishersSanFrancisco
A Division of HarperCollinsPublishers

First published in 1996 by Collins Publishers San Francisco,
1160 Battery Street, San Francisco, CA 94111
HarperCollins Web Site: http://www. harpercollins.com

©1996 CPI
Cover photograph by Ed Kashi
Back cover photograph by Cristina Garcia Rodero

Library of Congress Cataloging-in-Publication Data
Jerusalem, In the Shadow of Heaven / directed and edited by David Cohen
and Lee Liberman; text by Susan Wels.
ISBN: 0-00-225095-0
1. Jerusalem—pictorial works. 2. Jerusalem—Social life and customs—
Pictorial works. I. Cohen, David, 1955-
II. Liberman, Lee. III. Title.
DS 109.2. W45 1996
956.94'42—dc20   95-43359
                                        CIP

Design: Tom Morgan, Blue Design, San Francisco, California

Printed in Hong Kong. First printing 1996

10 9 8 7 6 5 4 3 2 1

This page: With the new headquarters of the Israeli Banking
Authority in the foreground, Jerusalem's New City is swathed in
morning mist. **Raghu Rai**

Previous page: Sunrise over the Augusta Victoria Hospital on
Mount Scopus. **Shai Ginott**

This book is dedicated to the memory of Yitzhak Rabin,
a citizen of Jerusalem and the world, a soldier for peace.

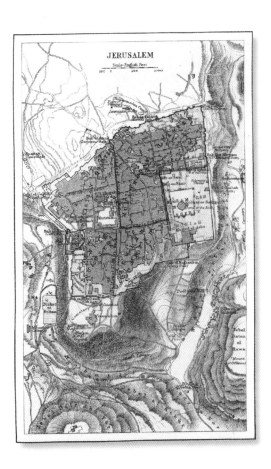

JERUSALEM

Glittering and solemn, born and reborn on the blood and ashes of her violent history, Jerusalem has roused the prayers and reverent longing of Jews, Christians, and Moslems for millennia. More than an earthly city crowning rough slopes at the edge of a desert wilderness, Jerusalem, Mountain of God, has been most of all a kingdom of faith and imagination. Her ancient sanctuaries, ramparts, and stony streets and houses are dusted with sanctity, a heavy mingling of myth and memory.

Jerusalem emerged as a great capital of faith three thousand years ago, when David captured the hilltop Jebusite stronghold and, dancing and shouting before the Lord, brought up to it the holy Ark of

Left: An area in the Kidron Valley just outside of Jerusalem's Old City. Photographed in the British Mandate period by Lionel Green. Above: Map of Jerusalem from The Family Bible, A. J. Holman & Co., 1882.

the Covenant. It was then that Jerusalem became not only the political seat of the young kingdom of Israel but the dwelling place of God. In the centuries that followed, Jerusalem became the battleground of rival creeds and nations vying to possess her holy places, too often banishing or slaughtering nonbelievers. The history of Jerusalem is a chronicle of zealous dreams and righteous bloodshed. Over and over again, the city and its people have been swept away—cleansed in the name of empire and religion, in the words of the Second Book of Kings, "as one wipes a dish, wiping it and turning it upside down."

Memories, however, have not been washed away in the successive waves of conquest. Instead, they have accumulated, layer on layer, like the city's crumbling stones.

The Rock at the Center of the World

Viewed from the Mount of Olives, across the sloping City of the Dead, Old Jerusalem rises in a tumult of battlements, towers, and pale, amber-colored roofs and houses. Ramparts rim the vast esplanade known to Jews as the Temple Mount and to Moslems as *Haram al-Sharif*, "the Noble Sanctuary." On this holy crest of Mount Moriah, where Solomon's Temple once stood, gleams the gold-crowned Dome of the Rock, one of the three holiest shrines in Islam. Inside the elaborate sanctuary, delicately tiled in Persian porcelain, is a barren rock, the epicenter of the city's spiritual conflicts and a sacred touchstone of three great religions.

At this bare outcropping, more than four thousand years ago, pagan Canaanites worshipped Shalem, god of the setting sun. It was here, later, that Abraham bound his son for sacrifice. Araunah the Jebusite used the rough limestone slab for threshing grain. He sold the rock to David, Israel's first king, for fifty silver shekels. On this gray stone, David built an altar and sacrificed to God, and here Solomon and Herod built their vaulted temples. In the seventh century C.E., after vanquishing the weakened Byzantines, Moslems raised their Dome of the Rock over the sacred stone, where believers hold Mohammed ascended into heaven. After Crusaders stormed the city in 1099, they built an altar to Christ over the rock and purloined fragments to sell as far away as Europe and Constantinople. The fabled "Foundation Stone" (*Even Ha-Shetiyah*), Jewish sages held, was the holy cen-

ter of the earth, the very spot where the world began. Beneath it, Moslems believe, is the awful well of souls awaiting the Last Judgment at the meeting place of heaven and the gates of hell.

An accumulation of belief clings not just to the Temple Mount but to nearly every brooding corner of Jerusalem. Its air, wrote the Israeli poet Yehuda Amichai, "is saturated with prayers and dreams/ like the air over industrial cities." Behind the Dome of the Rock, through a labyrinth of crooked streets and alleys, stands another, older sanctuary—the Church of the Holy Sepulcher. This shrine, too, encompasses a maelstrom of religious meaning. A Roman temple of Venus stood on this site when Queen Helena—mother of the first Christian emperor, Constantine—recognized it as the place of Christ's crucifixion and tomb in 326 C.E. The pagan temple was swiftly replaced by new, Christian, monuments. Over the course of some sixteen centuries, Christian pilgrims have journeyed to this great basilica to see not just the golden socket that held Christ's cross and the crypt where he was laid but the Stone of Unction where the Savior's body was anointed, the place of his flagellation, the spot that Christians believed was the very navel of the earth, and the tomb of Adam, the first man, whose skull was said to lie beneath the stones of Calvary.

Fire and Blood

Jerusalem has always been a city close to God. She has also been, for much of her history, a political backwater, "a city at the end of the road," in the words of Israeli novelist Amos Oz. No trade routes or waterways ran by her. Built on a stony ridge above a barren wasteland, Jerusalem towered over other cities only as a spiritual capital. Alexander the Great and Napoleon both ignored Jerusalem in their great campaigns to conquer the Levant. Even so, her streets have for tens of centuries been the front lines of holy conflicts between potent theological and cultural forces.

The city has been burnt and ruined by devastating sacks and sieges fifty times in thirty centuries. Over and over, often in the name of God, her streets have run with blood, and her temples have been razed into rubble.

David, the young warrior-king, first conquered the citadel in 1000 B.C.E. and made it the capital of his nation, which for the first time united the two southern tribes of Simon and

Judah with the ten northern tribes of Israel. When he brought to the city the holy Ark of the Covenant, the mobile shrine that contained Moses' tablets of the law, *Ir David*—the City of David—became the spiritual and temporal center of the Jewish people. David bought the threshing floor of Araunah on Mount Moriah, and his son, Solomon, built there the great Temple for the Ark, which he consecrated in 952 B.C.E.

Three and a half centuries later, the armies of the Babylonian king Nebuchadnezzar swept over Jerusalem, destroying Solomon's Temple and carrying the leaders of the city into captivity. Persia overpowered Babylon soon after, and many of the banished Jews returned to their ruined city, rebuilding its walls and constructing a second Temple. Jerusalem was restored to the Jews under Persian rule, until the armies of Alexander the Great crushed the Persian Empire in 332 B.C.E.

In the second century B.C.E., the Seleucid (Syrian Greek) king Antiochus IV took power and outlawed Jewish practice, on penalty of death. Antiochus transformed the Temple into a sanctuary of

Jerusalem, the **Bait al-Maqdis** *("site of holiness"), with its vast Temple Mount, crowns a rocky ridge above the Valley of Hinnom. This view was drawn by J. Archer in the mid-to late nineteenth century.*

Opposite page: The Dome of the Rock, the third holiest shrine in Islam, is built above the stone on which Abraham prepared his son for sacrifice.

Zeus and slaughtered swine across the holy altars. Within two years, his draconian rule had incited a Jewish War of Resistance, led by Judah Maccabee ("the Hammer") and his five brothers from the House of Hasmon. From their base in the barren Judean hills, the revolutionaries seized control of the Temple Mount and purified the sanctuary—an event commemorated in the Jewish holiday of Chanukah. Eventually, the Hasmoneans took control of the entire city, as well as Samaria, Judah, and the Galilee, and ruled independently until 63 B.C.E., when Jerusalem fell under Roman domination.

Cars and tourists crowd the Damascus Gate, the entrance to the Old City's Moslem Quarter, during the British Mandate period.

Soon after, in 37 B.C.E., Rome appointed the Idumean leader Herod as king of Judea. A paranoid ruler, Herod attempted to curry favor with the Jews by undertaking a vast reconstruction of the Temple. The colossal edifice he created—one of the wonders of the ancient world—was the Temple to which the twelve-year-old Jesus came with his family on pilgrimage. Its immense courtyards accommodated three hundred thousand worshippers. The wall supporting the great sanctuary, according to the first-century historian Josephus, was "the greatest ever heard of by man."

Herod died in 4 C.E., and in 66 the War of the Jews erupted against Roman rule. After years of struggle and a bloody, five-month battle for Jerusalem, the imperial forces under Titus smashed the Jewish revolt in 70. On the ninth day of the Hebrew month of Av—the same day on which Babylonian forces had destroyed Solomon's Temple—a Roman soldier set Herod's Temple afire, burning it to rubble only six years after it had been completed. Hundreds of thousands perished within the city walls. The carnage was so great, recorded the historian Josephus, that flames in the burning city were quenched with human blood.

In 132, the Emperor Hadrian outlawed Jewish observance in the ravaged city and declared that Jerusalem would be rebuilt as a Roman town. This ignited a second Jewish revolt—led by the general Simon Bar Kochba—and this time the rebels managed to seize and hold the city for three years. In 135, however, Hadrian attacked with forces from as far away as Africa and Britain, slaughtering more than half a million and obliterating a thousand Jewish settlements. After the revolt was brutally put down, Hadrian banned Jews from entering the city gates with the exception of one day a year—the ninth of Av—when they would be admitted to lament the destruction of their Temple. Jerusalem, renamed Aelia Capitolina, was rebuilt in four quadrants surrounded by walls—an arrangement that still exists today—and a shrine to Jupiter and Hadrian's statues were erected on the Temple Mount.

If I should forget thee, O Jerusalem, may my right hand forget its strength. May my tongue cleave to the roof of my mouth, if I do not set Jerusalem above my highest joy. **Psalms 137:5–6**

In 312, Emperor Constantine the Great converted to Christianity. Soon after, he pulled down the pagan temples and constructed the Church of the Holy Sepulcher—then called the Anastasis ("Resurrection") Church—and many other sanctuaries on sites identified as Christian holy places. Jerusalem was transformed again, this time into a flourishing center of Byzantine Christianity.

Three centuries later, however, the city and its churches once again lay in smoldering ruins—destroyed by Zoroastrian Persians who attacked in 614, slaughtering nearly thirty-five thousand people. Christians briefly regained control over Jerusalem, only to be overcome by Arab invaders who starved the city until its citizens surrendered. The Moslem reign they established—under the Umayyad, Abbasid, and Fatimid caliphs—lasted more than four centuries.

In November 1095, Pope Urban II called on Christians to wage a holy war to rescue Jerusalem from the Moslem "infidels." Thousands of peasants, townspeople, and noblemen joined the pope's Crusader army and headed for the Holy Land, pillaging towns and cities along the way in a bloody rampage of looting and violence.

In June 1099, Crusader forces reached Jerusalem. On July 15 the knights scaled the walls under torrents of arrows and a flaming mixture of oil and sulfur called Greek Fire. The week of carnage that followed rivaled the blood lust of the Romans a thousand years earlier. The soldiers of Christ slaughtered fifty thousand non-Christians in the city, murdering all of the Moslem men, women, and children who had taken refuge inside the Al-Aqsa Mosque and setting fire to the synagogue in which the Jews had gathered, seeking safety. The Christian victors, according to one witness, dripped with blood from head to foot; six months later, a visitor reported, the city still stank of rotting corpses.

For nearly a century, the Crusader kings reigned over Jerusalem as a Christian citadel, constructing churches and hospices for pilgrims throughout the city. In 1187, however, the Kurdish general Saladin laid seige to Jerusalem and restored it to Moslem rule without massacre or plunder. In the thirteenth century, control of the city passed to the Egyptian Mameluks—originally Turkish soldier-slaves who had risen to power under the Abbasid caliphs. In 1516, the Mameluks in turn were ousted by well-armed Ottoman Turks employing an effective new technology—muskets and gunpowder. The rule of the tax-hungry Ottomans lasted for four centuries, a period during which Jerusalem gradually descended into brutal poverty. Inhabitants scratched out a meager

A nineteenth-century artist's conception of the magnificent Temple built by Herod the Great in the first century B.C.E.

living from the city's small industries, soap making and the sale of religious souvenirs. Mark Twain, visiting Jerusalem in 1867, reported that "lepers, cripples, the blind and the idiotics assail you on every hand . . . Jerusalem is mournful and dreary and lifeless."

In 1917 the city was captured by British forces under the leadership of General Edmund Allenby. For the next three decades, the British governed Jerusalem and Palestine under a mandate granted by the League of Nations in 1921. When the British pulled out in 1948, competing Jewish and Arab claims over the territory erupted into war, culminating in a bitter, two-month siege of Jerusalem. When the fighting ended, the city was divided. The Old City and East Jerusalem were under Jordanian control, while West Jerusalem was held by the new state of Israel. In June 1967, Israeli forces captured the Arab sections of Jerusalem, unifying the city and bringing it under Jewish control for the first time in two thousand years. "The war is over," Israeli Defense Minister Moshe Dayan said, adding presciently, "Now the trouble begins."

A City United, A City Divided

In the City of David, unification has not in any sense translated into unity. Jerusalem is torn today, as she has been throughout her history, by adverse religions, ideologies, and national groups. There are no more barricades and minefields carving up the city, but there is an invisible dividing line between East and West Jerusalem. The lives of Jews and Arabs rarely intersect; each group clings to its own neighborhoods and animosities. The city's Christians, too, now a population in decline, have a long history of often bloody squabbling and infighting. In the Church of the Holy Sepulcher, portions of which are controlled by fractious orders of Greek Orthodox, Armenian, Latin, Syrian, Coptic, and Ethiopian ecclesiastics, fights still break out—as they have for centuries— over such territorial issues as which group has claim to a particular staircase or the right to sweep a dusty corner of the basilica. In the seventeenth century, an Englishman visiting the church reported that the Christian sects fought with so much "unchristian fury and animosity" over the control of the sanctuary that "they have sometimes proceeded to blows and wounds even at the very

In you is my Paradise and my Hell;

and in you is my reward and my punishment.

And blessed is he who visits you!

Again, blessed is he who visits you!

Again, blessed is he who visits you!

al-Fazari, THE BOOK OF AROUSING SOULS
[early fourteenth century]

door of the sepulcher, mingling their own blood with their sacrifices." In the nineteenth century, Moslem troops were necessary to keep the peace among the Christians inside the church—today, the duty is assigned to Israeli police officers.

As in ancient times, Jerusalem's Jews, too, are split into antagonistic factions. The numbers of the city's ultra-religious *Haredi* ("God-fearing") Jews are increasing rapidly, thanks in part to a prolific birth rate. The black-garbed fundamentalists rant against the city's secular Jews as heretics and apostates, and they excoriate each other in posters plastered on the walls of their communities. In recent years, the fundamentalists have asserted a powerful, sometimes violent influence over the city's life, which they are determined to cleanse of ungodly distractions. Sirens blaringly announce the Jewish *Shabbos* on Friday afternoons. In some parts of the city, outraged religious vigilantes have hurled stones at drivers who violate the Sabbath bans and torched bus shelters featuring advertisements of immodestly dressed women.

All this conflict, all this history of savage competition, has imbued Jerusalem with a defensive, fortresslike quality. The massive, medieval battlements and walled religious enclaves, the hulking structures of the newly rebuilt Jewish Quarter, and the colossal pre-1967 housing developments that shot up on the city's edge—with outer walls triple the normal thickness and machine guns stationed on their roofs—heighten the tense atmosphere of a city still under siege, tormented by forces menacing a fragile peace.

Old, unforgiven wounds do not heal in the emotionally charged air of Jerusalem—a city where, observed the poet Amichai, "the numbers are not of bus-routes/ but: 70 After, 1917, 500/ B.C., Forty-Eight. These are the lines/ you really travel on." Memories of war are sharp. Rusting hulks of tanks and armored cars, destroyed in the 1948 War, line the road into the city. Bullet holes from 1967 pockmark the walls of houses on the edge of East Jerusalem. As recently as twenty years ago, a border wall abruptly severed Jaffa Road; beyond the wall were streets and shops that were unreachable and almost unimaginable to citizens who had never been allowed to venture past the neighborhood frontier. Still today, Jerusalem remains endlessly at conflict within itself.

Of Paradigms and Pilgrims

There has always been a dissonance between the ideal, divine Jerusalem and the gritty reality of the holy city. Jerusalem gained miraculous qualities in the backward glances of her religious exiles. To the Jews, banished time after time from their sacred capital, a utopian Jerusalem existed miles up in the heavens. On the day of resurrection, sages declared, the city and her great Temple would descend from the skies like a pillar of fire, blazing brighter than the sun and moon. Throughout the Diaspora, the catastrophic loss of Zion, David's city, has been ritually remembered. Prayers are said, facing Jerusalem, three times a day. A section of every home is left unpainted, a piece of jewelry remains unworn, bridegrooms smash a goblet underfoot during the wedding ceremony—all to recall the destruction of the Temple and the pain of life without Jerusalem.

A view of the Temple Mount, or Haram al-Sharif, from the Mount of Olives, drawn in the nineteenth century by W. M. Craig for a Boston publisher.

Christians also conceived of a New Jerusalem that was infinitely more perfect than the earthly city. In the Book of Revelation, Jerusalem is envisioned "coming down from out of heaven from God, made ready like a bride adorned for her husband," shining with divine glory, with twelve angels stationed on her gates. To the Moslems, too, who lost Jerusalem to the Crusaders, the city from afar assumed new religious stature. "The greatest of places is Jerusalem, and the greatest of rocks is the Rock of Jerusalem," declared a *hadith*, a traditional saying attributed to the Prophet. Moslem pilgrims who set out for Jerusalem, it was said, would be attended by ten thousand angels who would intercede and pray for them. On the Day of Judgment, the great shrine of Mecca itself would miraculously descend onto Mount Zion in Jerusalem, the *Bait al-Maqdis* ("site of holiness").

The contrast between the glorious Jerusalem of the imagination and the congested and contentious earthly city has always been more than some visitors can handle. Pilgrims in the past were known to succumb to a strange, psychotic illness known as Jerusalemite

Inside the Damascus Gate, whose ornate upper structures were built by Suleiman the Magnificent in the sixteenth century. Photographed in the British Mandate period by Lionel Green.

fever. Even today, Kfar Shaul Psychiatric Hospital specializes in treating victims of a temporary insanity called Jerusalem Syndrome that exclusively afflicts religious tourists to the city. Sufferers may be found wandering the city dressed in bedsheets, convinced they are the messiah, Samson, or the Virgin Mary, and lodging complaints when hotels won't honor their request for the Last Supper.

For many more, however, a visit to Jerusalem is a powerful affirmation of faith, a geographic link to the religious past. "Jerusalem is the source," wrote one observer. "It is the heart and the spirit, the soul and the oversoul." Since the beginning of the city's history, pilgrims have journeyed to Jerusalem as a sacramental obligation. When the great Temples still stood, hundreds of thousands of Jews would travel to the capital three times a year to celebrate the Hebrew festivals of Passover; Shavu'ot, the Feast of Weeks; and Sukkot, or Tabernacles—the largest of the feasts, referred to as the hagg (a term that later metamorphosed into *hajj*, the Arabic word for pilgrimage to Mecca). After 70 C.E., Jerusalem became the focus of intense longing for her exiles. Jews continued to enter the city on the ninth of Av to mourn the Temple and to weep over Jerusalem from the distant summit of the Mount of Olives. Bribes to Roman officials sometimes enabled them to visit the sacred Western Wall and other holy places; some even settled again inside the city. In medieval times, displaced Jews continued to return to Zion. Rabbi Benjamin of Tudela, who journeyed from Spain to Jerusalem in the middle of the twelfth century, reported visiting "the Western Wall, one of the walls which formed the Holy of Holies of the ancient Temple; it is called the Gate of Mercy, and all Jews resort thither to say their prayers."

By the late 1800s, great numbers of Jews were making their way back to Jerusalem—swelling the Jewish population from six thousand to thirty-five thousand in the last half of the cen-

tury and expanding into new neighborhoods beyond the city walls. The Zionist vision of reestablishing a Jewish state in Eretz Israel took root, and successive waves of immigrants from Europe and Yemen made *aliyah* to the holy land. In the words of one young Israeli paratrooper who fought to regain Jerusalem in 1967, the ancient capital is "the source, the cornerstone of the whole Jewish people."

For Christians, Jerusalem was only a political capital during the brief century of Crusader rule, but the city has been a spiritual center of the faith since the middle of the fourth century C.E. By the fifth century, Jerusalem had become a crowded "metropolis of Christendom," where Christians of all nations flocked to worship, day and night, at scores of Byzantine churches and monasteries. The pilgrims carried home with them souvenirs of the holy sites—bits of stone, bone, drops of holy oil from Christian shrines, and splinters of the True Cross, which they surreptitiously bit off when they kissed the holy relic. Great numbers of the pilgrims, in actuality, were criminals who struck out on the arduous journey to Jerusalem as penance for their crimes and arrived in the city without a trace of piety, feigned or otherwise. Throughout the Middle Ages, vast numbers of pious folk as well as "parricides, perjurers, . . . dice players, mimes and actors" made the *peregrinatio ad loca sancta*, spawning a brisk business in translators, guides, provisioners, and other tourist services.

The pilgrims visited all the popular holy places, particularly the Way of the Cross and the Holy Sepulcher—a sanctuary in which they spent considerable time, since visitors were locked inside by Saracen guards for twenty-four-hour periods. Aside from hosts of fleas and the noisy carousing of less observant visitors, pilgrims suffered little during their long stay inside the church, since it was filled with shops and bazaars hawking food and goods ranging from Pater Noster beads to precious silks and damasks. In the nineteenth century, the city was flooded by devout and destitute Russian peasants, who walked thousands of miles to Jerusalem from the most distant corners of their country. Today, Jerusalem still fills with Christian visitors during Easter week and other holy festivals. Seeing and touching the physical geography of Christ's life and reenacting his Passion along the stony Way of Sorrows, they reconnect themselves with the history and spirit of their faith.

Jerusalem has long been a holy destination for Moslem pilgrims, too; each year tens of thousands travel to the city, often en route to or from the sacred shrine at Mecca. In the earliest days of Islam, worshippers faced Jerusalem three times a day during prayer, as did the Jews. Although Mohammad eventually instructed his followers to face Mecca instead, prayer in Jerusalem was said to be worth five hundred prayers said elsewhere. Whoever made pilgrimage to Jerusalem and prayed there five times a day was declared purified of guilt. Jerusalem was considered holy because it was said to be the location of the "farthest mosque," where the Prophet began his Night Journey into heaven to receive Allah's final revelation. Moreover, it was in Jerusalem, according to Moslem lore, that the Resurrection would take place on the Day of Judgment; the dead would cross the Valley of Jehosophat, below the *Haram,* to be judged by God.

Today, the city is a center of longing for Palestinians—Moslem and Christian—who were displaced by the conflicts of 1948 and 1967. "Do you know Jerusalem?" wrote the Palestinian writer Jabra Ibrahim Jabra. "How beautiful the olive groves were in Talbiyya, Qatamon and Musallaba! How beautiful was the valley that stretched all the way to Maliha! It was there that we left part of our lives as a gift, as a pledge that we would return."

3001 and Beyond

"If anything," observed the Israeli writer Amos Elon, "Jerusalem is a city loved too well yet never quite wisely." And, today, the question of the "future status" of the city hovers like a cloud over Jerusalem's new shopping malls, industrial parks, museums and galleries, and expanding neighborhoods. Long treasured for its ancient, lustrous beauty and religious eminence, Jerusalem has reinvented itself, since 1967, as a vital center of Israel's civic and cultural life. But the political and economic stability of the city, now the largest in Israel, is menaced by the competing, uncompromising claims of its various citizens. Jerusalem, a growing metropolis on the brink of late-twentieth-century prosperity, risks becoming, once again, an isolated fortress on the edge. Unified or again officially divided, a theocracy or secular capital: the only thing certain about Jerusalem's future is that it will be built, like her walls, on the bright dreams and unforgiving wreckage of the past.

What follows are the photographic observations of more than fifty of the world's foremost photographers, who were set loose in Jerusalem on a fine spring day. Their pictures capture Jerusalem's turbulent past and its rich diversity, its architectural splendor, fierce passions and spiritual intensity. They also give some clue as to why the sages wrote, "Ten portions of beauty descended to the world. Jerusalem acquired nine."

This sixteenth-century map shows Jerusalem as the center of the world, surrounded by the continents of Europe, Africa, and Asia.

A thirteenth-century illumination depicts the twelve gates of the heavenly Jerusalem.

JERUSALEM

3000 Years of History

 1000 BCE

Canaanite and Jebusite period—from 2500 B.C.E.

c. 1000 B.C.E.—Jerusalem captured by King David. Solomon consecrates the First Temple in 952.

PERIODS OF SOVEREIGNTY

▬	JEWISH/ISRAELI
▬	PERSIAN
▬	GREEK/PTOLEMAIC
▬	SYRIAN
▬	ROMAN
▬	MOSLEM
▬	CRUSADER
▬	OTTOMAN (TURKISH)
▬	BRITISH

198 B.C.E.—The Seleucid king Antiochus III conquers Judea, which becomes a tributary of Syria.

164 B.C.E.—The Jews, under the Maccabees (Hasmoneans), defeat the Syrians, reconsecrate the Temple and eventually rule Jerusalem, Samaria, Judah, and the Galilee.

500

332—Byzantine Emperor Constantine begins construction of the Church of the Holy Sepulcher and other Christian sites in Jerusalem.

614—Brief period of Persian rule begins. Churches destroyed and thirty-five thousand slaughtered.

1000

1071—Seljuk Turks capture Jerusalem.

1099—Crusaders capture Jerusalem. Fifty thousand Moslems and Jews are slaughtered.

00 BCE

586 B.C.E.—Jerusalem captured by Nebuchadnezzar of Babylonia. City is destroyed.

539 B.C.E.—Cyrus the Great of Persia conquers Babylonia. Jews are allowed to return to Jerusalem and to build the Second Temple.

332 B.C.E.—Alexander the Great adds Jerusalem to his empire.

312 B.C.E.—Ptolemy I of Egypt, one of Alexander's former generals, rules Palestine.

63 B.C.E.—Rome conquers Palestine and later sets up the House of Herod.

c. 30 C.E.—Crucifixion of Christ in Jerusalem.

70—Second Temple destroyed by Romans. Western ("Wailing") Wall remains.

135—The Bar Kochba revolt is subdued. Five hundred thousand are killed. Jews are banished from Jerusalem, which is renamed Aelia Capitolina.

638—Moslems take Jerusalem six years after the death of Mohammed.

691—Dome of the Rock is built.

1500

1187—Saladin captures Jerusalem for the Moslems. The Ayyubid and Mameluk dynasties follow.

1244—Jerusalem sacked by Mongols.

1516—The Ottoman Empire takes over Palestine and Jerusalem.

2000

1917—After Ottoman defeat in WW I, British Mandate period begins.

1947—Under the United Nations partition plan, Jerusalem is declared an international city. After the 1948 War the city is divided between Jordan and Israel.

1967—Israel captures all of Jerusalem in the Six-Day War. Jerusalem is under Jewish rule for the first time in more than two thousand years.

Stone dwellings and
sanctuaries of the Old City
gleam in the rosy light of
dawn. In the foreground is the
Mount of Olives, the largest
and oldest Jewish cemetery in
the world, dating back to
biblical times.

Rick Rickman

Following pages: The aroma of
fresh baguettes, pita, Arab
bagels, and Sephardic *biscochos*
draws early morning shoppers
to the Chava brothers bakery
in the popular Mahane Yehuda
market on Jaffa Road.

Nik Wheeler

Previous pages: A worker
polishes the golden crown of
the Dome of the Rock on the
Temple Mount. The new 24-
karat dome was commissioned
in 1993 by King Hussein of
Jordan, who has served as the
official custodian of
Jerusalem's Islamic holy sites.

Nick Kelsh

An Arab mule driver makes
his way among Jewish tombs
on the Mount of Olives.
Stones are left by visitors upon
the graves as tokens of
remembrance.

C. W. Griffin

Previous pages: A young worshipper enters the ornate Cathedral of St. James in the Old City's Armenian Quarter. According to tradition, the church dates to the fourth century, when it was named for Jesus' brother James, the first bishop of Jerusalem. James was stoned in 62 C.E., and his body is said to be interred under the cathedral's main altar. Also buried inside the church is the head of the brother of St. John the Apostle, who was slain by Herod's son, Agrippa, in 44 C.E.

Nubar Alexanian

Lifelong study of the scriptures is a hallmark of Jerusalem's traditional Jewish communities. Scholars of all ages fill hundreds of simple, street-corner synagogues and storefront Torah schools.

Daniel Lainé

Despite clinging to the dress and traditions of eighteenth-century eastern European *shtetls*, ultra-Orthodox Jews, including residents of Jerusalem's Mea Shearim enclave, take full advantage of modern telephone, fax, and computer technologies. A free dial-in phone service called "Dial-a-Daf," for example, broadcasts hour-long Talmud lessons to callers every sixty minutes around the clock.

Daniel Lainé

Jeans hang out to dry amid the crumbling stone of the Old
City's Arab Quarter, where families make their homes inside the
ancient walls.

Nina Barnett

Clerical vestments stand ready in the sacristy of the Dominican
Church of St. Stephen, near the Damascus Gate, where Father
José Loza, a Mexican priest, prepares for Sunday mass.

Pascal Maitre

At the huge Mahane Yehuda farmer's market, Jerusalemites shop for inexpensive fresh fruits and vegetables. In Jerusalem's highly politicized atmosphere, Mahane Yehuda is considered by some to be a haven of right-wing sentiment.

Nik Wheeler

A quiet moment between customers in the Old City's Arab Market.

Paul Chesley

Opposite page: The Tamimi Bakery in the Anata refugee camp turns out trays of fresh pita bread for local Arab families. A thousand Palestinians reside in the camp, which includes several schools, a clinic, markets, and small shops. Many of the families originally abandoned their homes in Jerusalem and the surrounding areas during the 1948 War. Since that time, the growing refugee population has received much of its relief aid from the United Nations.

Jane Evelyn Atwood

In the middle of morning mass, a priest is framed in the altar window of Dominus Flevit Church on the Mount of Olives. The present church was built by the Franciscans in the early 1950s on the site where, according to tradition, Jesus wept before entering the city of Jerusalem. Like many of the city's holy sites, Dominus Flevit ("the Lord wept") stands atop layers of earlier, ruined sanctuaries, including a Crusader church and a fifth-century monastic chapel.

C. W. Griffin

Opposite page: Young boys listen to an early-morning lecture before heading off to school in the gentrified Jewish Quarter of the Old City. Since 1967, Israelis have restored ruined buildings in the once destitute neighborhood near the Western Wall and constructed new homes, schools, and synagogues. Some five hundred Jewish families now reside in the expanded quarter.

Ed Kashi

A young Arab mechanic patches up a fender in the Wadi Joz
neighborhood of East Jerusalem between the city and Mount Scopus.

Miki Kratsman

Stones and phones line an ancient street in the Old City's Jewish Quarter.

Ed Kashi

At the monastery of St. John
outside Ein Karem, Father
Laurent, a Greek Orthodox monk
from France, painstakingly restores
seventeenth-century Russian icons
that will be sold to other churches.
Ein Karem is the site of more than
a dozen Christian churches,
monasteries, and convents.

Pascal Maitre

Following pages: Long-bearded
Haredim pray and study at the
Western Wall, a remnant of the
retaining wall of the great Temple
platform constructed by Herod
the Great in 20 B.C.E. Since the
Temple was destroyed by the
Romans in 70 C.E., Jews have
gathered at the Wall to mourn the
loss. Sitting on the scholar's table
is a *shofar*—the ram's horn that is
sounded during the Jewish high
holy days of Rosh Ha-Shanah and
Yom Kippur. The blowing of the
shofar was banned at the Wall by
Moslem authorities from 1931 to
1948, and Jews were excluded
from the Wall altogether after the
1948 War. The shofar was once
again sounded at the Wall after
the Israelis recaptured the Old
City in 1967.

Pascal Maitre

From their perch atop the city walls near the Damascus Gate, Israeli border police scan the crowd in the packed Arab Quarter market.

Joel Sartore

Following pages: The shimmering Dome of the Rock—erected in the seventh century on Mount Moriah where the Temple of Solomon once stood—towers over the mazelike streets of the Old City. Until the mid-1800s, Jerusalem's mosques were, by Ottoman decree, among the tallest structures in the city. Today, the skyline is dominated by the office buildings and hotels of the New City.

James Marshall

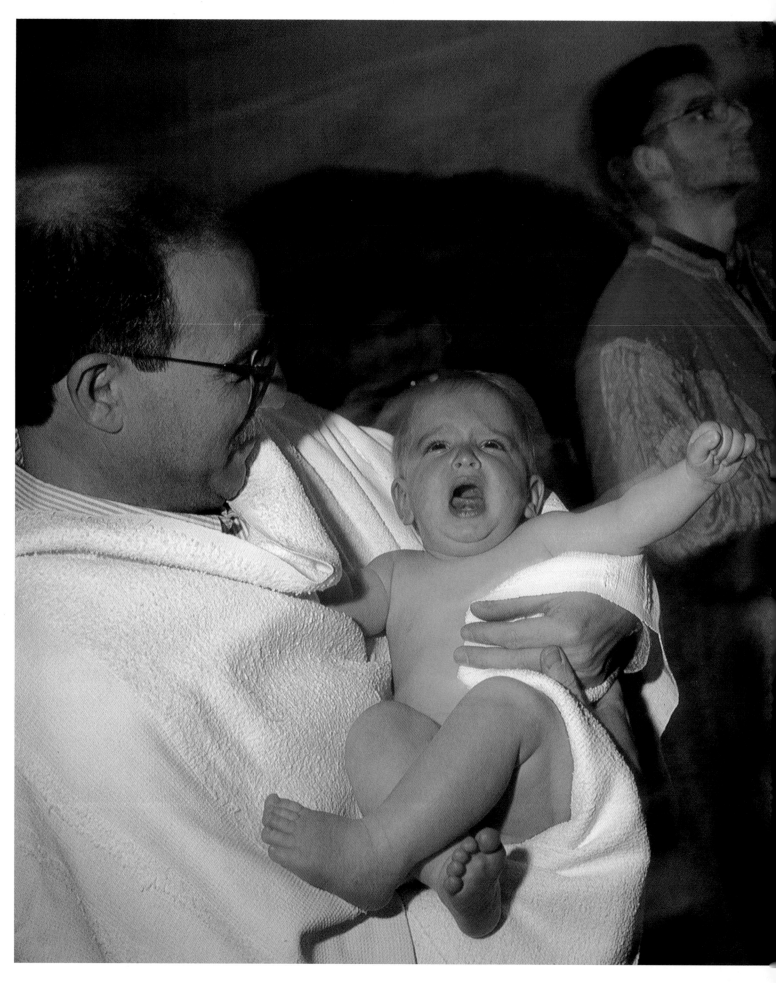

An Armenian family from
Hungary brings their baby to
be baptized at the Convent of
the Archangels in the Armenian Quarter of the Old City.
Armenians have been present
in Jerusalem since the early
fourth century, after the
kingdom of Armenia became
the first nation to convert to
Christianity in 301. Today the
quarter is a guarded enclave
of tranquil gardens and
monastic buildings inhabited
by some two thousand clergy
and laypeople.

Nubar Alexanian

Following pages: Monumental
stained-glass windows by
the late Mordechai Ardon,
interpreting the Prophet
Isaiah's vision of the End of
Days, illuminate the Israeli
National Library at the Hebrew
University in Givat Ram.

Barry Frydlender

Schoolboys pose with bright new toys in Abu Ghosh, an Arab village
west of the city. A century ago, Abu Ghosh was the last caravan stop
for pilgrims traveling to Jerusalem, and wayfarers were required to pay
a toll to pass through the town. More than three thousand years ago,
according to both Jewish and Christian lore, the Ark of the Covenant
was kept here before King David carried it to his new capital of
Jerusalem. Modern-day Abu Ghosh is famous for what is arguably the
best hummus in Israel.

Raymond DeMoulin

Opposite page: An Ethiopian Christian monk rests in front of one of the
rough-hewn huts constructed on the roof of the Church of the Holy
Sepulcher. A community of Ethiopian Christian monks has lived on the
sanctuary's roof since they were exiled there in one of many, sometimes
bloody, clashes among the six Christian sects that occupy the legendary
basilica.

Michael Coyne

Constructed in 691 C.E. by Caliph Abd el-Malik, the Dome of the Rock *(Qubbat el Sakhra)* surrounds the sacred Moriah stone on which Abraham prepared to sacrifice his son. The same limestone rock is thought by some to be the location of the Holy of Holies, the most hallowed sanctum of Solomon's Temple, and Moslems believe it to be the spot from which Mohammed ascended to heaven on his steed, al-Buraq. The inner walls of the sanctuary are covered with carved and painted marble, Byzantine mosaics, and inscriptions from the Koran.

Cristina Garcia Rodero

A cross stands in a crude window on the roof of the Church of the Holy Sepulcher.

C. W. Griffin

Fresh-picked strawberries at the Mahane Yehuda market.

Rick Rickman

Opposite page: Twelve-year-old Achinoam Mashmoor accepts a
rose and proud hug from her father, Nissim, after completing her
Bat Mitzvah at Jerusalem's Hebrew Union College. The coming-
of-age ceremony at Hebrew Union, a center of Reform Judaism
in Israel, was performed by Rabbi Na'ama Kelman, Israel's first
female rabbi.

Nina Barnett

Near the Church of the Holy Sepulcher in the Old City's Christian Quarter, Sister Almonda (left) and Sister Sofia care for boys in the orphanage of St. Saviour Church, a Franciscan complex built in 1559.

Sylvia Plachy

Opposite page: New immigrants start over on the Ben Yehuda pedestrian mall. More than half a million Jews from the former Soviet Union have made *aliyah* to Israel since 1989.

Paul Chesley

Masses of Israelis crowd the plaza in front of the Western Wall on Jerusalem Day, a spring holiday celebrating Jerusalem's unification by the Israeli army during the Six-Day War. Israelis captured the Old City on the twenty-eighth day of the Hebrew month of Iyar in 1967. Immediately after, soldiers cleared Arab dwellings from the area in front of the wall, where Jews had been banned from worshipping for nearly two decades. They created a vast plaza that has since been used regularly for religious and state occasions. A famous aspect of the annual Jerusalem Day celebration is the Jerusalem march, which draws tens of thousands of participants from dozens of countries.

Paul Chesley

The luminous beauty of Jerusalem results, in part, from the use
of local stone in all its buildings—an architectural feature that
has been required by law since the British Mandate began in
1917. At Castle Marble Industries, workers transport twenty-ton
blocks of Jerusalem stone—a distinctive mix of limestone and
chalk—from a nearby quarry in Hebron.

Photographs by Scott Thode

An Arab mason chisels blocks of the soft white stone, which weathers into shades of amber, gray, and rose.

The rough-grained stone—called *mizi yahudi*, *mizi ahmar*, or *mizi hilou*, depending on its color—is cut at the Castle Marble plant.

Meir Pedros gazes at his one-year-old pet hawk, Rumba, which he has raised since it was a hatchling. Pedros, his wife, Iris, and their dog, Sensemilia, live with 176 other low-income Israeli families at a caravan site in Givat Hamatos in the southern part of Jerusalem. The camp also functions as an absorption center for hundreds of new immigrants from Ethiopia and the former Soviet Union.

Lori Grinker

In the Jewish Quarter of the Old City, a reconstructed arch of the destroyed synagogue, called *Hurva* ("the ruin"), conveys the monumental grace of the sanctuary it once adorned. The original synagogue was begun in the eighteenth century, finished in the mid-nineteenth century, and destroyed by the Jordanian army in 1948.

Claus C. Meyer

Like countless Christian pilgrims who traveled to Jerusalem before
them, these worshippers, bearing crosses, retrace the legendary
footsteps of Christ along the Via Dolorosa to Golgotha (Mount
Calvary) inside the Church of the Holy Sepulcher. Although the
fourteen Stations of the Cross along the route bear little if any
relationship to the historical path that Jesus actually followed to his
crucifixion, the reenactment of Christ's suffering can be, for many
Christians, a powerful reaffirmation of their faith.

Photograph by Cristina Garcia Rodero

A pilgrim, imagining Christ's agony, crawls along the stony footpath of the Via Dolorosa, called the Way of Sorrows.

Photograph by Cristina Garcia Rodero

Tourists and pilgrims explore
the site of Christ's crucifixion,
one of many shrines within
the Church of the Holy
Sepulcher, which is divided
among frequently fractious
Greek Orthodox, Latin,
Armenian, Coptic, Syrian, and
Ethiopian Christian sects. The
original church—constructed
in the fourth century by the
Emperor Constantine—was
rebuilt by the Crusaders in the
eleventh century.

Gerd Ludwig

At Yeshivat Hakotel, a center for advanced Torah study in the
Old City, students noisily debate sections of the Talmud, the
written corpus of Jewish law.

Raghu Rai

Excited third-graders tackle English lessons at the Jabil Mukaber Charity School, where 312 Islamic students pay $150 a month for a private education. East Jerusalem's public schools are closed as many as ten days a month due to the political strikes that, for years, have paralyzed public life in the Arab sections of the city. The Jabil Mukaber school is usually closed only once a month.

Susan Meiselas

Before attending a town-planning session dealing with the
construction of a large new Intel electronics plant in Jerusalem,
Mayor Ehud Olmert (center) consults with noted Jerusalem
attorney Naomi Weil, who represents the corporation. In recent
years, Jerusalem has sought to bolster its economic base by
attracting foreign high-tech and science-based companies. Some
industrial expansion plans, however, have been halted by
advocates who favor developing available land into housing,
especially near the city's fast-growing Orthodox communities.

David Rubinger

Opposite page: Mayor Olmert pays a visit to young constituents
in a Jerusalem kindergarten class.

David Rubinger

PORTRAITS OF THE OLD CITY

by Anthony Barboza

The gold-capped Dome of the Rock blazes in Jerusalem's midday sun. In the first centuries after its construction, the dome was draped with animal skins in winter to shield it from the damaging effects of wind and snow.

Michael Coyne

Just east of Jerusalem stretches
the barren wilderness of the
Judean Desert, where Jesus
wandered for forty days
seeking spiritual renewal.
Since ancient times, hermits
and austere religious sects
have retreated to its forbidding
hills and caves.

Robert Holmes

Following pages: The Shrine
of the Book, in the Israel
Museum complex, houses
some of the two-thousand-
year-old Dead Sea Scrolls,
discovered in 1947 in a cave at
Qumran near the Dead Sea.
The paleo-Hebrew scrolls—
most of them written in the
first century B.C.E. by the
Essenes, an ascetic Jewish
sect—include an ancient copy
of the Book of Isaiah, the
oldest existing complete
biblical text. The Shrine of the
Book is built in the shape of
the covers of the earthenware
jars in which the Dead Sea
Scrolls were found.

Paul Chesley

Initiation into the study of
Torah—the first five books of
the Bible—is an occasion
worth celebrating in
Jerusalem's traditional Jewish
communities. These five-
year-olds, whose party
crowns read *Mesibat Chumash*
("Five Books of Moses
party"), have mastered their
aleph-bet and are ready to
begin the Book of Genesis.

Daniel Lainé

An Old City sweet shop
overflows with tempting
heaps of Turkish delight,
baklava, pistachios, dried
fruit, and other Middle
Eastern delicacies.

James Marshall

Sacramental candles illuminate a prayer niche in the Church of
the Holy Sepulcher.

Claus C. Meyer

To avoid being photographed—a breach of the second command-
ment against graven images—a black-jacketed *Haredi* Jew hides
his face on a Mea Shearim street.

Daniel Lainé

Sheikh Abdul-Aein Salhad, director
general of the Islamic Waqf, Grand
Mufti, and spiritual leader of the

Abbess Anna of the Russian
Ecclesiastical Mission Orthodox
monastery

Rabbi Moshe Hirsch, "the foreign
minister" of Naturei Karta, the most
extreme Orthodox community

Abuna Matthewos, archbishop of
the Ethiopian Orthodox Church

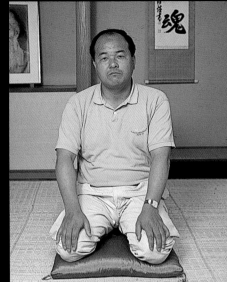

Hanoch M. Fujii, director of the
Japanese Christian Makoya Center

Diodorus I, patriarch of the
Greek Orthodox Church

Archbishop Dionysius Behnam
Yacoub Jajjawi, Syrian Orthodox
Patriarchal Vicar in the Holy Land

Archbishop Abraham of the
Coptic Orthodox Church for
Jerusalem and the Near East

Dennis Jenkyns, representative of Jerusalem's Baha'i Church

Kas Raphael Hadana, representative of the Ethiopian Jews in Jerusalem

Sheikh Abdallah Nimr Darwish (center), spiritual leader of Jerusalem's Islamic Movement

Father Theodosius, representative of the Russian Ecclesiastical Mission

Reform Rabbi Na'ama Kelman, director of education for the Israeli Progressive Movement

A bride and her young attendant hurry to the *kotel*, the Western Wall, to pray for a blessing on her wedding day. According to Jewish custom, women are separated from men at the wall by a *mechitsah,* or screen, to reduce distractions during prayer.

Hana Sahar

Previous pages: *Haredi* children hide their eyes to ward off photographs.

Hana Sahar

While Mordechai Arbibo says his morning prayers, his wife, Tamar, stands in the doorway of their home in Katamon, a posh Arab neighborhood before the 1948 War. During the siege of Jerusalem, residents of the Jewish Quarter were evacuated to Katamon and its environs. It became, in large part, a poor Jewish neighborhood and the adjacent area of Gonen was characterized by drab apartment blocks and high crime rates. Recently, however, the grand old Arab houses have been regentrified by Israeli yuppies.

Eldad Rafaeli

Opposite page: A young celebrant carries Israeli flags for Jerusalem Day.

Nick Kelsh

Narguila (water-pipe) smoking regulars spend hours over backgammon and cards at East Jerusalem's Al Rawdah Cafe.

Susan Meiselas

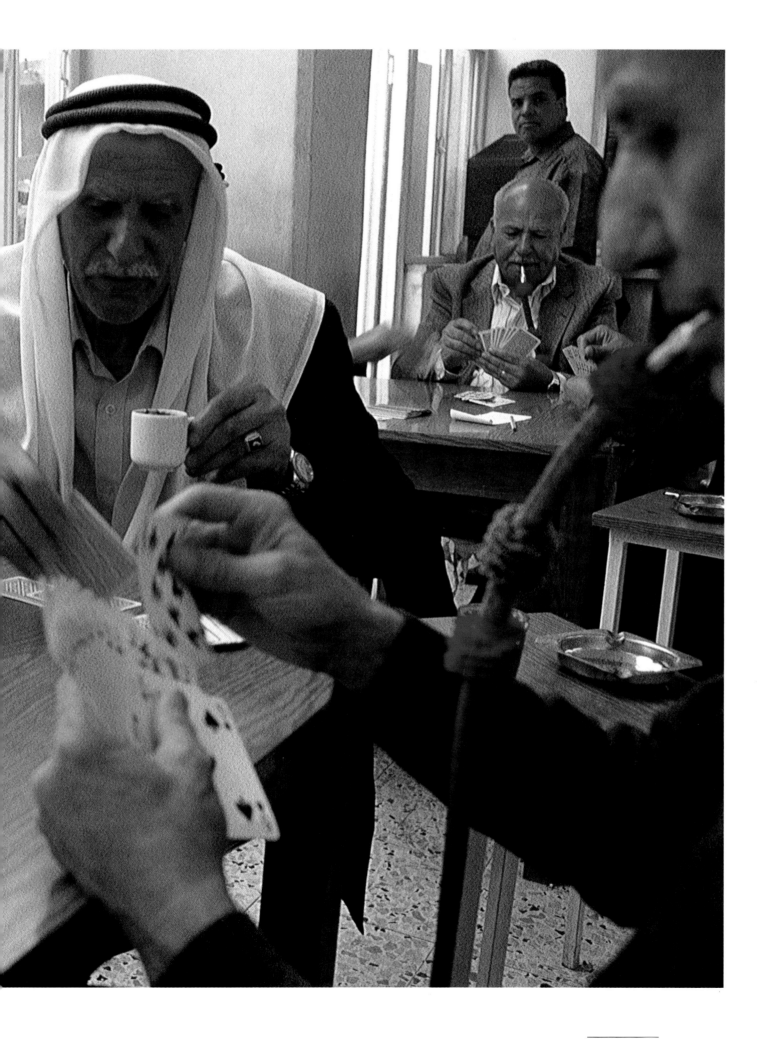

On Kibbutz Ramat Rachel, a collective farm in southern Jerusalem, South African *kibbutzniks* Darren Kalish (left) and Stefan Bellon ride out to the farm's apple orchard to clear stones from the freshly planted field. Despite its peaceful, pastoral appearance, Ramat Rachel, founded by ten pioneers in 1926, suffered heavy casualties and damage during the fighting between 1948 and 1967, when it was on the border between Israel and Jordan. Today, three hundred adults and children make their home on the kibbutz, which features a hotel, sports center, kindergarten, clinic, chicken houses, and apple and cherry orchards.

Acey Harper

A volunteer sorts through stocks of crutches and wheelchair equipment at Yad Sarah, Israel's largest charitable organization. Hundreds of thousands of Jewish and non-Jewish elderly and disabled borrow medical and orthopedic equipment free of charge from Yad Sarah, whose volunteers assemble and renovate the devices. The organization also provides meals, laundry, transportation, and emergency services for Jerusalem's seniors.

Leonard Freed

Differences in Jewish practice stand out in sharp relief at the Western Wall, a gathering place for the black-garbed Orthodox as well as for secular Jewish tourists.

Paul Chesley

No longer useful as transport in late-twentieth-century Jerusalem, camels are a curiosity for kids and camera-toting tourists.

Hana Sahar

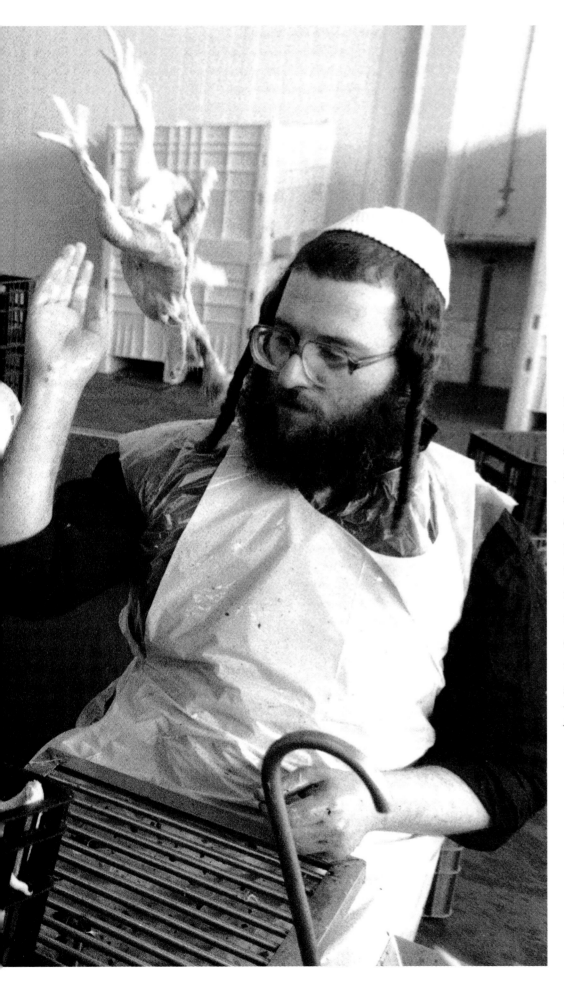

Every Orthodox community maintains its own kosher slaughterhouse, where *shochatim u-vodkim* ("ritual slaughterers and checkers") ensure that animals are properly butchered according to Jewish law. In Atarot, a northern suburb of Jerusalem, rabbis and shochets check chickens for impurities, tossing away undesirable birds as *treyfah* (forbidden food).

Alon Reininger

Great white pelicans strut along the grassy shore of a man-made pond, complete with waterfalls and monkey islands, at Jerusalem's new Biblical Zoo in the Malcha neighborhood.

Shai Ginott

Following pages: The Migdal David, the imposing citadel that overlooks the Jaffa Gate, has somehow survived the city's waves of conquest and destruction. Its earliest structures date from the Hasmonean dynasty—successors of the Maccabees—in the second century B.C.E. The fortress complex was later expanded to protect an adjacent royal palace of Herod the Great, and it was occupied by the Roman Tenth Legion after the destruction of Jerusalem in 70 C.E. It was, in fact, the only structure in the city left standing after the Roman carnage. The Crusader kings made the citadel their stronghold and placed its image on their coins. The present fortress was built by Mameluk rulers in the fourteenth century. After Israel unified the city in 1967, the citadel became the site of the new Museum of the City of Jerusalem.

Claus C. Meyer

Artin Sesserian, an Armenian Christian, pauses inside the Church
of the Holy Sepulcher. The sixty-four-year-old Jerusalemite
resides in the Old City, where Armenians have lived relatively
peacefully for nearly seventeen hundred years.

Razi Robinowitz

Before a backdrop of the Dome of the Rock, a portrait photographer poses inside his studio in the Old City's Arab Quarter.

Razi Robinowitz

A souvenir vendor hawks menorahs, beads, and olivewood mementos from his mobile display in the Old City. Religious trinkets have been big business in Jerusalem ever since large numbers of pilgrims began making their way to the holy city. One enterprising Jerusalem shop, popular with pilgrims around 600 C.E., manufactured a line of souvenirs decorated with crosses for Christian customers and identical keepsakes festooned with menorahs for the city's Jewish visitors.

Paul Chesley

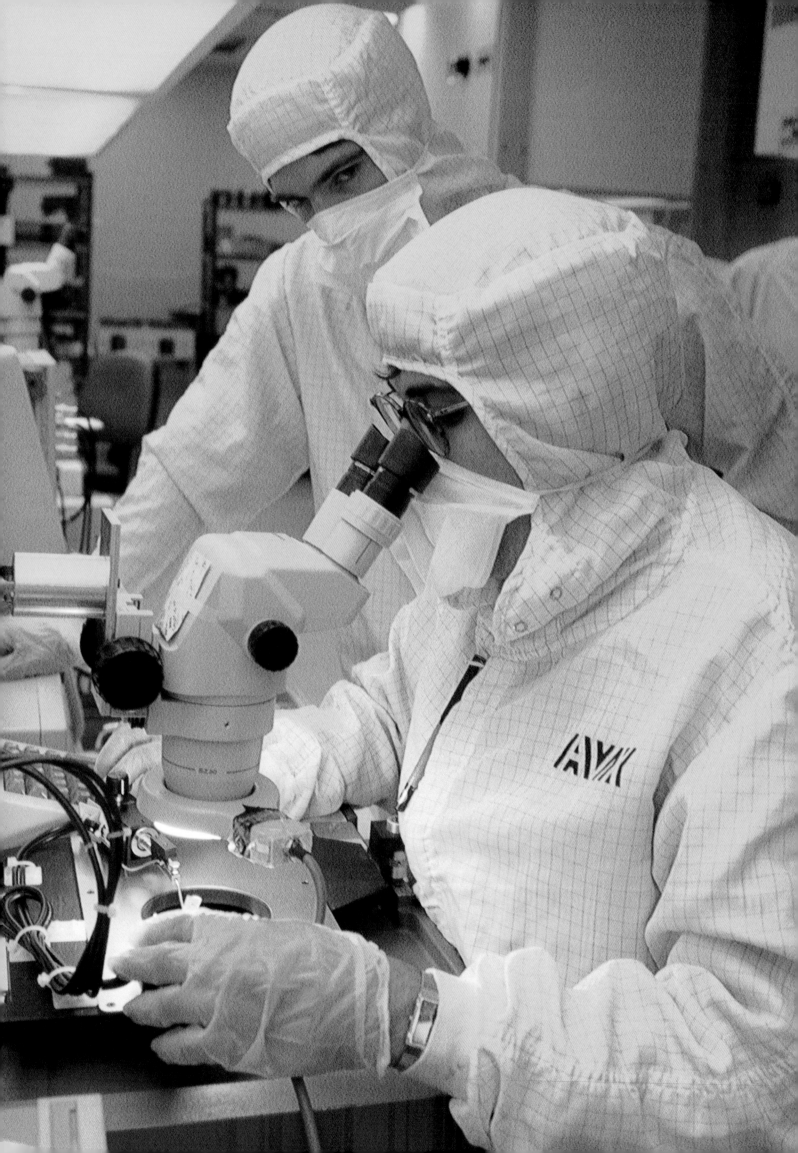

In the Church of St. Stephen near the Old City, Father Jean
Michel looks after the monastery's extensive collection of old
cameras and photographs of nineteenth-century Jerusalem. The
Dominican complex also houses the hundred-year-old library
and museum of the French Institute for Biblical Archaeology.

Pascal Maitre

Opposite page: Jerusalem's improved infrastructure, new industrial parks, and financial incentives have persuaded many high-
tech companies—such as AVX Israel, an electronics firm—to
locate their manufacturing and research operations in the city.

Eldad Rafaeli

Ethiopian Christians worship in their large New City church built in
the nineteenth century. Ethiopians have long maintained historic
and religious ties to the city, which they trace to the Queen of Sheba's
journey to Jerusalem to test the wisdom of King Solomon.

Jeffery Allan Salter

Haredi students hang their hats and coats under a plaque
commemorating donors to their school, the Hasidic *Etz Chaim*
("Tree of Life") yeshiva.

Nik Wheeler

Following pages: Father Laurent prays in a grotto chapel of the
monastery of St. John in the Desert near Ein Karem. According to
the gospel, John the Baptist spent his youth in this hilly region,
which was known as the First Desert of St. John.

Pascal Maitre

Vines cling to the rough walls of the monastery of St. John in the Desert.

Pascal Maitre

Opposite page: Little girls giggle over the railing of their honeycomb-shaped apartment building in Ramot Polin, a new neighborhood built after the 1967 Six-Day War. The avant-garde housing units, constructed in the 1970s, were unpopular from the time they were built and are now filled with large ultra-Orthodox Jewish families looking for inexpensive housing.

Shabtai Tal

A priest hurries past a pizzeria
on the Via Dolorosa.

C. W. Griffin

The Damascus Gate, the most beautiful of the seven portals in the city's walls, provides a lofty lookout over the Arab Quarter. Its foundations were built by the Romans under Herod, while its upper structures—like most of the Old City's perimeter walls—were rebuilt by the Ottoman ruler Suleiman the Magnificent in the mid-sixteenth century.

Joel Sartore

Following pages: A couple strolls through Sacher Park near the Knesset.

Shai Ginott

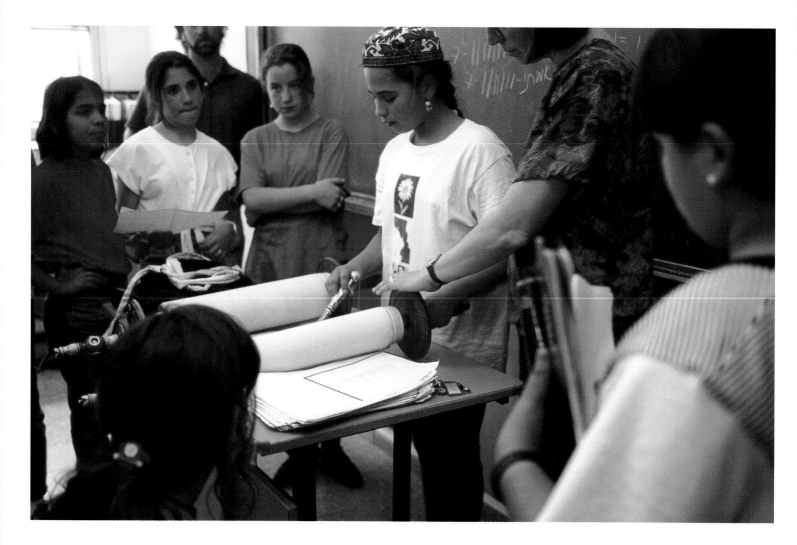

In preparation for their Bat Mitzvahs, girls at Jerusalem's Progressive (Reform) Tali School practice reading sections of the Torah under the direction of Rabbi Na'ama Kelman.

Nina Barnett

Near Jerusalem's central bus station, soldiers sprawl in the shade
before boarding military buses to travel to their posts in various
parts of Israel. Able-bodied, eighteen-year-old Israelis are required
to enter the armed forces. Men must serve in the Israel Defense
Forces (IDF) for three years, and women serve twenty months.

Larry Price

PORTRAITS OF EAST JERUSALEM

by Carol Guzy

Play grimly imitates reality in the East Jerusalem neighborhood of Kalandia, where young Arab boys with toy pistols play a local version of "cowboys and Indians," staging mock shoot-outs between Palestinians and Israeli soldiers.

Nine-year-old Amal Atta relaxes for a moment between classes at an Arab Christian girls' school in the Palestinian village of Beit Hannina, outside Jerusalem.

Eager young students vie for a teacher's attention at the Beit Hannina girls' school.

After school in Kalandia, Palestinian children relax with their mother, a journalist and teacher, while she fixes a meal for the next day.

Five days after his release from Ramla Prison, Abrahim Muhana, forty-six—a leader of Al-Fatah—begins life at home again in Jerusalem with his family of six children. Muhana, who had been imprisoned for ten years, was released as a direct result of negotiations between Israeli and PLO authorities.

James Marshall

A *Haredi* couple poses at home with their five children. The political power of the city's ultra-Orthodox Jews is rising quickly, due in part to their high birthrate. Seven or eight children per family is the norm. As a result, *Haredi* kids account for more than half of all the city's Jewish children under the age of ten.

Daniel Lainé

As part of their military education, Israeli soldiers visit Yad Vashem, Israel's monument to the Nazi Holocaust. The memorial complex is built atop Mount Herzl, whose slopes are covered by a military cemetery.

Rick Rickman

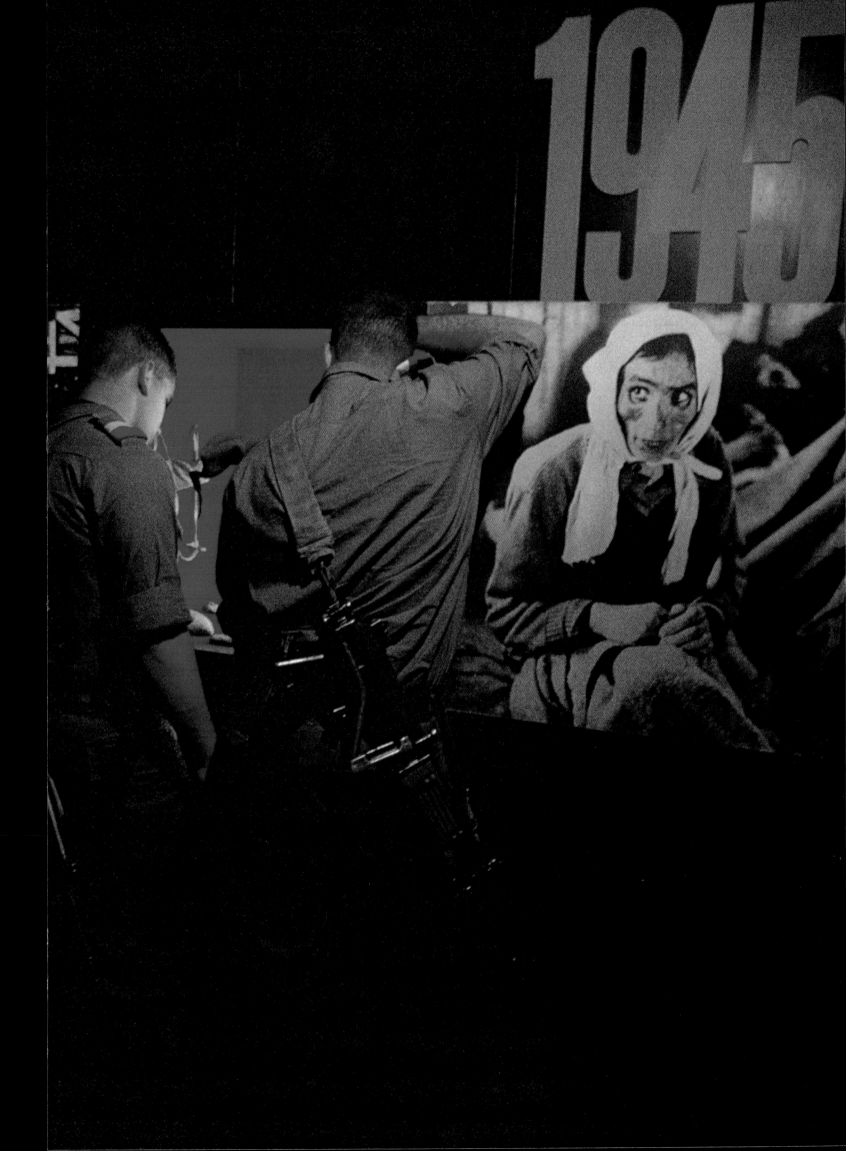

The late Prime Minister Yitzhak Rabin (fourth from left), who
also served as Israel's Minister of Defense, presided over a 9 A.M.
cabinet meeting in his government offices near the Knesset.

David Rubinger

Opposite page: Meir Shamgar, former president of Israel's
Supreme Court—which monitors the nation's legislative and
executive activities—stands in an arched corridor of the new
Supreme Court building overlooking the Knesset, Israel's house
of representatives.

Shlomo Arad

At a reception on the eve of Jerusalem Day, the city's mayor, Ehud Olmert (left), the late Prime Minister Yitzhak Rabin (center), and Jerusalem's former longtime mayor Teddy Kolleck gathered to commemorate the historic unification of the city in 1967. On November 4, 1995, Rabin, 73, was assassinated by a right-wing Jewish gunman who opposed the landmark peace accord that the prime minister had brokered with the Palestinians.

David Rubinger

Following pages: A Bedouin treks across the barren Judean hills that stretch from the eastern borders of the city.

Robert Holmes

Boisterous Jerusalem Day
celebrants parade past Arab
shopkeepers in the winding
alleys of the Old City.

Gerd Ludwig

Following pages: Inexpensive
housing and a central location
near the Mahane Yehuda
market have made the
Nahalat Zion neighborhood a
popular address.

Avi Ganor

Yitzhak Giladi, a painter and
art gallery owner in the
renovated Jewish Quarter,
comes home to share a midday
meal with his wife, Bella, and
their six children.

Ed Kashi

After their wedding ceremony at the Ethiopian church in the New
City, Delensahu Zewdia and his bride, Berehane Jegne, stop for
photos and an impromptu celebration on the Haas Promenade,
which overlooks the Old City from the Hill of Evil Counsel.

Nick Kelsh

Opposite page: To commemorate the city's liberation, Orthodox
students march in prayer from their yeshiva on Mount Zion to
spend the night at the Western Wall.

Miki Kratsman

In a pigeon roost inside the Old
City's Arab Quarter, twenty-
two-year-old Muhammed
Gulani cares for the thirty-five
varieties of pet birds he has
kept since he was a boy.

Susan Meiselas

High school dancers warm up backstage before a Sunday night performance at the Tower of David Museum in the Old City.

Anthony Barboza

Opposite page: Twenty-month-old Juliette Asfoor gazes solemnly at the walls outside the Church of the Holy Sepulcher. The Arab Catholic child is gowned in white as a symbol of her dedication to the Virgin Mary.

Cristina Garcia Rodero

Sipping glasses of tea and
black coffee, religious Jewish
men pass the time at a
card club.

Nik Wheeler

Previous pages: Jerusalemites
unwind after work with Jewish
folk dancing in a city gym.

Rick Rickman

Orthodox Christians gather for
Sunday morning prayers
inside the Church of the Holy
Sepulcher.

Gerd Ludwig

Shortly before he died on August 18, 1994, at the age of 91, Yeshayahu Leibowitz, an acclaimed and controversial Jewish philosopher and professor at Jerusalem's Hebrew University, posed in his Rehavia study. An outspoken critic of Israel's policies in the occupied territories, Leibowitz was praised by President Ezer Weizman as "a spiritual conscience for many in Israel."

Michal Heiman

Following pages: Religious graffiti stains a wall in the Old City's Arab market.

Paul Chesley

As a blessing each evening at
sunset, a nun carries an icon
of the Madonna and child
around the walls of the
Gorninska Convent in Ein
Karem. The convent served as
a hospice for Russian pilgrims
who journeyed in great
numbers to the Holy Land,
often on foot, at the end of the
nineteenth century.

Marina Yurchenko

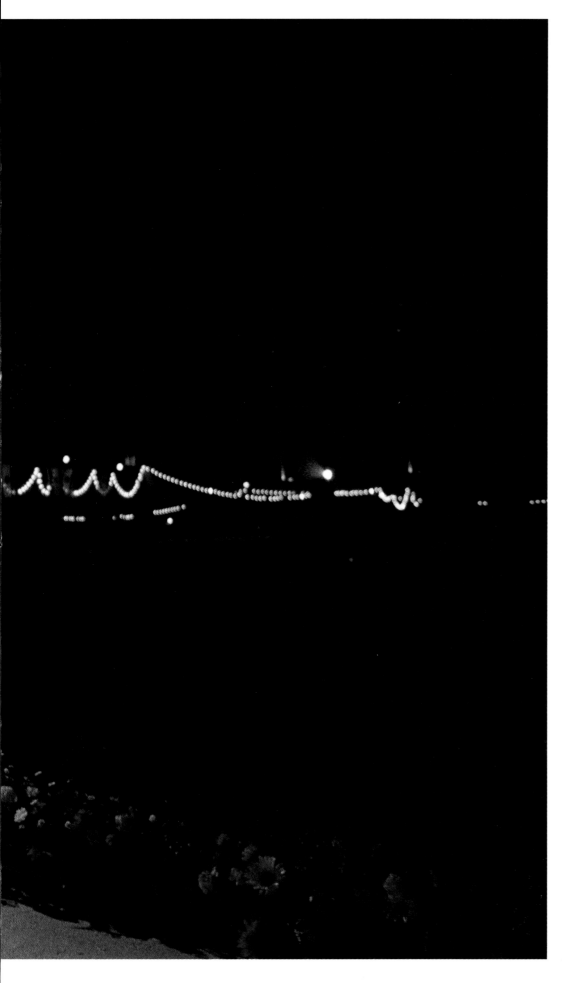

Mayor Ehud Olmert addresses
a crowd of twenty-five
hundred who have gathered
for a reception on the eve of
Jerusalem Day.

David Rubinger

Following pages: The sun
hovers over neighborhoods
of the New City.

Joel Sartore

The City Tower office building dominates the Nachlaot neighborhoods.

Robert Holmes

Following pages: The lighting in the courtyard of the Migdal David shows off the fourteenth century Mameluk ruins.

Tal Gluck

Sculptor Ran Morin prunes
seventy-year-old olive trees
growing atop his monument,
"Olive Columns," near the
Ramat Rachel kibbutz.

Micha Bar'Am

Photographers

Nubar Alexanian, USA

Shlomo Arad, Israel

Jane Evelyn Atwood, France

Micha Bar'Am, Israel

Anthony Barboza, USA

Nina Barnett, USA

Rick Browne, USA

Paul Chesley, USA

Michael Coyne, Australia

Barbara D. DeMoulin, USA

Raymond DeMoulin, USA

Leonard Freed, USA

Barry Frydlender, Israel

Avi Ganor, Israel

Cristina Garcia Rodero, Spain

Shai Ginott, Israel

Yehoshua Glotman, Israel

Tal Gluck, Israel

C. W. Griffin, USA

Lori Grinker, USA

Carol Guzy, USA

Acey Harper, USA

Michal Heiman, Israel

Robert Holmes, UK

Ed Kashi, USA

Nick Kelsh, USA

Antonin Kratochvil,
   Czech Republic

Miki Kratsman, Israel

Hiroji Kubota, Japan

Daniel Lainé, France

Vera Lentz, Peru

Gerd Ludwig, Germany

Pascal Maitre, France

James Marshall, USA

Susan Meiselas, USA

Claus C. Meyer, Brazil

Sylvia Plachy, USA

Larry Price, USA

Eldad Rafaeli, Israel

Raghu Rai, India

Alon Reininger, USA

Rick Rickman, USA

Razi Robinowitz, Israel

Steve Rubin, USA

David Rubinger, Israel

Hana Sahar, Israel

Jeffery Allan Salter, USA

Emmanuel Santos, Australia

Joel Sartore, USA

Shabtai Tal, Israel

Scott Thode, USA

Nik Wheeler, UK

Marina Yurchenko, Russia

Memo Zack, Israel

Project Staff

Directors and Editors

David Cohen

Lee Liberman

Text

Susan Wels

Director of Photography

Peter Howe

Design

Brenda Eno and Tom Morgan
at Blue Design

Assignment Research

Lee Liberman

Assignment Coordinator

Alona Vardi

Sponsorship Director

James Marshall

Finance Director

Devyani Kamdar

Production Coordinator

Barry Sundermeier

Logistics Coordinator

Linda Lamb

Production Assistants

Joshua Liberman

Cassy Liberman

Berry Liberman

Post-Production Manager

Jain Lemos

Picture Editors

David Cohen

Sandra Eisert

Peter Howe

Lee Liberman

Copy Editor

Jeff Campbell

Research Consultants

Gil Havov

Michael Jankelowitz

Dan Prath

John F. Rothmann

Alona Vardi

Attorneys

Deborah Adelsky

Philip Feldman

Joshua Rosensweig

Photographers' Biographies

Nubar Alexanian
American/Boston, Massachusetts
Alexanian is a documentary photographer whose work has been widely published in the *New York Times Magazine, Life, Fortune, GEO,* the *London Sunday Times,* and others. His first book, *Stones in the Road: Photographs of Peru,* was published in the United States in 1994. His second book, *Where Music Comes From,* was published in the fall of 1995. He has received numerous awards, including a Fulbright Fellowship in 1983 for work in Peru. Alexanian found the best falafel he ever had across from the Fifth Station of the Cross in Jerusalem.

Shlomo Arad
Israeli/Tel Aviv
A professional photographer for twenty-eight years who has concentrated on coverage of conflicts in the Middle East, Arad has been published widely in the Israeli press as well as in major European and American publications, such as the *New York Times Magazine, Stern, VSD,* and numerous others in Sweden and Great Britain. He was *Newsweek's* contract photographer in Israel for fifteen years. In 1974, he was awarded the Anna Rivkin Bruck Prize and held a one-man exhibition in Tel Aviv. His photographs have appeared in many international exhibitions, and his photo album, *Bedouins: The Sinai Nomads,* was published in Tel Aviv in 1984.

Jane Evelyn Atwood
American/Paris
Jane Evelyn Atwood was born in New York in 1947 and has been living in France since 1971. A member of Contact Press Images since 1988, she works primarily in the tradition of documentary photography following individuals or groups of people—usually those on the fringes of society—for long periods of time. She is the author of three books—two about French prostitutes in Paris and one about the French Foreign Legion. She has won various international prizes and was the first recipient of the W. Eugene Smith Award in 1980 for her work on the blind. In 1987, she won a World Press Prize for *Jean-Louis—Living and Dying with AIDS.* In 1990, she received the *Paris Match* Grand Prix du Photojournalisme and in 1991 was granted the Canon Photo Essay Award for her work in women's prisons in the former Soviet Union. Her first retrospective, *Documents,* was part of the Mois de la Photo in Paris in 1990–91.

Micha Bar'Am
Israeli/Ramat Gan
An active photographer since the 1950s, Bar'Am has been associated with Magnum Photos since 1967 when he teamed up with Cornell Capa to cover the Six-Day War. Bar'Am was a contract photographer for the *New York Times* from 1968 until 1992. He is a member of the International Center of Photography's International Advisory Council and he has been published and exhibited widely in Israel and abroad. Bar'Am's latest prize is the Israel Museum's Photography Prize for 1993. Bar'Am is the founding curator of the Photography Department at the Tel Aviv Museum of Art. He has a great beard.

Anthony Barboza
American/New York
Barboza began his photographic career in 1964 with the Kamoinge Workshop, under the direction of the revered African American photographer Roy DeCarava. His work has been published in the *New York Times Magazine, Life, Newsweek, Time, National Geographic, TV Guide, Elle, Vogue, US, McCall's, Vanity Fair, People, Details, Esquire, GQ, Harper's Bazaar, Self, Glamour, Woman's Day, Cosmopolitan, Playboy, Ms., Interview, The Village Voice, Ebony, Essence, Black Enterprise, Jet, Emerge,* and *GEO.*

Nina Barnett
American/New York
Barnett is a freelance editorial photographer based in Manhattan, her hometown. Photography is a second career. Previously, Barnett edited photography books for eight years. After switching careers, her first major assignment was for *A Day in the Life of America* in

Since the eighteenth century, Jews have crammed crevices in the Western Wall with bits of paper on which they've written fervent prayers, hopes, and pleas for divine intervention. Attendants collect "God's mail" monthly and ritually bury it in holy soil. Joel Sartore

1986. Currently, Barnett does feature work for the *New York Times Magazine, Money, Fortune, Seventeen,* and Whittle Communications, among others.

Rick Browne
American/Scotts Valley, California
Codirector of *Hong Kong: Here Be Dragons, A Day in the Life of Thailand,* and *Planet Vegas,* Browne is a photojournalist specializing in travel photography and environmental portraiture for both editorial and corporate clients. He recently received the silver medal from the Society of American Travel Writers. Browne has also been under contract as photographic consultant to the world-renowned Monterey Bay Aquarium.

Paul Chesley
American/Aspen, Colorado
Chesley is a freelance photographer who has worked with *National Geographic* since 1975, traveling regularly to Europe and Asia. He has completed more than thirty-five projects for the society. Solo exhibitions of his work have appeared in museums in London, Tokyo, and New York. *A Day in the Life of Israel* was the eleventh *Day in the Life* project for Chesley, a frequent contributor to *Life, Fortune, Time, Newsweek, Audubon, GEO,* and *Stern.* Recent books including his work are *The Circle of Life, Mauritius, Hawaii, Colorado,* and *America: Then & Now.*

Michael Coyne
Australian/Melbourne
Michael Coyne worked for eight years documenting the Iranian revolution, during which time his work appeared in a twenty-eight-page spread in *National Geographic*

and was featured in other magazines such as *Newsweek, Life, Time, German Geo,* and the *London Observer.* For his work in the Middle East he has received a number of awards, including two from the National Press Photographers Association and the Overseas Press Club of America. His two very successful books on Australia, *The Oz Factor* and *A World of Australians,* have resulted in national and international awards. Kodak Asia Pacific published a calendar of his Australian work in 1993, which won an international award for design. The National Museum of Australia curated a complete collection of the photographs from his latest book, *A World of Australians.* Coyne has been a contract photographer with the Black Star picture agency since 1985.

Barbara D. DeMoulin
American/Fort Worth, Texas
DeMoulin has been a fine portrait photographer for the last ten years, achieving the Masters level in the Professional Photographers of America. Her work has been published in several books, including *At the Rim,* a book on women's collegiate basketball, and shown in numerous exhibitions.

Raymond DeMoulin
American/Forth Worth, Texas
An honorary photographer on this project, DeMoulin is known as "Saint Ray" to photographers everywhere for his support of photography during his thirty-nine years at Eastman Kodak Company.

Leonard Freed
American/New York
Leonard Freed began his professional career as a painter, but within a short time, he became a photojournalist. He has worked regularly for the *London Sunday Times,* the *New York Times Magazine, Stern,* and *GEO,* traveling to all corners of the world. He has produced major essays on Poland, Asian immigration to England, North Sea oil development, violence in New York City, and Spain since Franco, among many other diverse projects. Recent essays include *Vendetta in Crete, Turkish Village, Cyprus, East Germany, Gambling in Atlantic City, Lebanon at War, Death of Black Children in Atlanta, Georgia,* and *The US Army in Germany.* He has received grants from the New York State Council on the Arts and the National Endowment for the Arts.

Freed's photographs, first exhibited in 1960, have been included in numerous exhibitions, including *The Concerned Photographer* series at the Riverside Museum in New York, the Smithsonian Institution in Washington, the National Museum in Jerusalem, and the Matsuya in Tokyo. Books featuring Freed's photographs include *Deutsche Juden Heute, Black in White America, Seltsamespiele, Made in Germany, Berlin,* part of Time-Life's *Great Cities of the World* series, *Police Work,* and *La Danse Des Fideles.*

Barry Frydlender
Israeli/Tel Aviv
In 1984, Frydlender received the Gerard Levy Prize from the Israel Museum in Jerusalem. One-man exhibitions of his work have been held at the Nikon Gallery in London, the Israel Museum in

Jerusalem, and the Photography Center of Athens. His work has been included in group shows in London, Jerusalem, New York, Tel Aviv, Helsinki, and Berlin.

Avi Ganor
Israeli/Ramat Hasharon
Ganor was born in 1950 in Ramat Hasharon, Israel. He studied aeronautical engineering at the Technion in Haifa before traveling to the United States to study at the San Francisco Art Institute, the Pratt Institute, and the Parsons School of Design in New York. Since 1977, Ganor has been working as a photographer and teaching at the Bezaiel Academy of Art and Design in Jerusalem, Beit Zvi in Ramat Gan, and Camera Obscura in Tel Aviv. Since 1991, he has been head of the department of computerized images at Camera Obscura.

Cristina Garcia Rodero
Spanish/Madrid
Garcia Rodero specializes in fine-art photography. Her work has been published in several magazines, including *Lookout* and *El País.* Previously a drawing teacher, she now teaches photography at the Facultad de Bellas Artes de la Universidad Complutense de Madrid, where she first studied Spanish fiestas, customs, and traditions. In 1985, she was awarded the Premio Planeta de Fotografía. Her book, *Espana Occulta,* is widely admired by photographers around the world.

Shai Ginott
Israeli/Tel Aviv
Born in 1958 in Jerusalem, Shai Ginott is widely recognized as one of Israel's most talented "new photographers," with several

published books to her credit. Ginott has served as director of photography at the Israel Nature Reserves Authority. Between 1985 and 1989, she was a guest lecturer at the Israel Professional Photographers' Association; Cambridge University; Hadassah College, Jerusalem; the University of Tel Aviv; the Hebrew University, Jerusalem; and the Ben-Gurion University of the Negev. In 1989 she was named "Best Nature Photographer" by *Israel Photographic Magazine*. Shai Ginott's clients include the Israel Defense Forces, *Land and Nature, Eretz,* El Al Airlines, Israel Ministry of Tourism, *Ma'ariv* (weekend supplement), the Jewish National Fund, and the *Jerusalem Post*. A traveling exhibit of her photographs, *Nature and Landscape in Israel*, commissioned by the Israel Foreign Ministry, is currently on display in several countries around the world.

Yehoshua Glotman

Israeli/Maale Hagalil

Yehoshua Glotman was born in 1953 in Israel. He has studied photography in Jerusalem and at the Polytechnic of Central London in England. His involvement with photography encompasses both fine-art photography and documentary work. Glotman has taught at the Bezalel Academy of Art in Jerusalem for the past eleven years. He has exhibited his work in Israel and Europe and is the author of *An Israeli's Album* (1988). He is now living in a small village in the upper Galilee with his wife and two children.

Tal Gluck

Israeli/Tel Aviv

A freelance photographer based in Israel, Tal Gluck has spent the last twelve years traveling around the world on assignment for major geographical magazines in Europe. He is the editorial photographer for the Israeli geographical magazine *Masa Acher*. Exhibitions of his work are currently appearing in Japan, Germany, and Israel.

C. W. Griffin

American/Miami, Florida

C. W. Griffin is a staff photographer for the *Miami Herald*. He also teaches advanced photojournalism at the University of Miami. His work has appeared in *Newsweek, National Geographic, Smithsonian,* and the books *Songs of My People* and *The African Americans*. His work has been recognized by the National Press Photographers Association, which named him Military Photographer of the Year in 1980. He is the only African American ever to win this award.

Lori Grinker

American/New York

Lori Grinker began her career in 1980, while still a student at Parsons School of Design, when an assignment about a young boxer was published as a cover story by *Inside Sports*. At that time, she met fourteen-year-old Mike Tyson, whom she has continued to photograph through the years. Her work has taken her to the Middle East, Southeast Asia, Eastern Europe, the former Soviet Union, Africa, and throughout the United States. She is particularly interested in the dramatic political and social changes now going on in Cambodia and Vietnam, where she has been traveling extensively since February 1989. Her photographs have been exhibited in museums and galleries in Paris, Amsterdam, Arles, and New York and have been featured in *Life,* the *New York Times Magazine, Newsweek, People,* the *Sunday Times Magazine* (London), *Stern, GEO,* and *Il Venerdi.*

Grinker has been a member of Contact Press Images since 1988. Her book, *The Invisible Thread: A Portrait of Jewish American Women* (1989), is an intimate collection of photographs exploring the diverse experience of Jewish women in the United States. A collection of images from the book toured the United States from 1990 to 1992. She is currently at work on two new book projects. One deals with indigenous peoples and their sacred relationship to the environment. The other, *When the War's Not Over,* studies the effects of war on veterans around the world.

Carol Guzy

American/Washington, DC

Carol Guzy was born in Bethlehem, Pennsylvania, in 1956. She lived there until 1978 when she completed her studies at Northampton County Area Community College, graduating with an associate's degree in registered nursing. A change of heart led her to the Art Institute of Fort Lauderdale in Florida to study photography. She graduated in 1980 with an associate in applied science degree in photography. While at the Art Institute, she interned at the *Miami Herald*. Upon graduation she was hired as a staff photographer. She spent eight years at the newspaper before moving to Washington, DC, in 1988 and starting as a staff photographer with the *Washington Post,* where she is presently employed. Her assignments include both domestic and foreign stories. She is a member of the National Press Photographers Association and the White House News Photographers Association. She has been honored with numerous awards, including the prestigious Pulitzer Prize in Spot News photography. She was twice named Photographer of the Year by the National Press Photographers Association.

Acey Harper

American/Tiburon, California

Acey Harper is a freelance photographer based in Tiburon, California. He has traveled worldwide for such clients as *People, National Geographic,* and *USA Today*. He is currently managing director of Reportage Stock.

Michal Heiman

Israeli/Tel Aviv

Born in Tel Aviv in 1954, Michal Heiman studied photography at Hadassah College in Jerusalem from 1977 to 1979. From 1982 to 1984, she studied painting and sculpting at the Art Teachers College in Ramat Hasharon. From 1984 to 1991, she worked as a freelance newspaper photographer, specializing in portrait photography. In 1992–93, Heiman was curator of Camera Obscura Gallery in Tel Aviv and taught at the School of Film and Television in Jerusalem, Camera Obscura, and the Hadassah Canadian WIZO College of Design in Haifa. She continues to curate the Camera Obscura Gallery and lecture in the School of Film and Television, Jerusalem, and Camera Obscura, Tel Aviv.

Robert Holmes

British/Mill Valley, California
Robert Holmes is one of the world's foremost travel photographers. He was the first person to receive the Society of American Travel Writers' Travel Photographer of the Year award twice, in 1990 and 1992. His work regularly appears in major travel publications, including *National Geographic, GEO, Travel & Leisure,* and *Islands.* He has fifteen books in print. His photographs have been exhibited widely and are included in both corporate and museum collections.

Ed Kashi

American/San Francisco, California
Ed Kashi is a freelance photojournalist based in San Francisco whose work has appeared in *National Geographic, Time, Fortune, GEO, Life, Smithsonian, London Independent Magazine, Newsweek, Forbes,* and the *New York Times Magazine,* among many other publications. He has dedicated the past three years to *National Geographic,* shooting cover stories on the Kurds, water problems in the Middle East, and the Crimea.

The story on the Kurds, which Kashi researched and proposed to the *Geographic,* took him to Iraq, Iran, Syria, Turkey, Lebanon, and Germany for eight grueling months in refugee camps and bombed-out Kurdish villages. It was published in book form by Pantheon in 1995. Kashi won a 1991 National Endowment for the Arts grant for his documentary work on the Loyalist community in Northern Ireland. These photos represent three years of personal work and have been published in the United States, Britain, Spain, Sweden, Japan, Canada, and Italy.

On the Day of Judgment, according to Jewish tradition, the Messiah will raise the dead on the Mount of Olives—and for this reason, a vast necropolis has covered its now treeless slopes, overlooking the Old City, since ancient times. Some seventy thousand Jewish graves crowd the hillside where Jesus wept over the city and where, for centuries, exiled Jews, barred from entering the city walls, gazed in prayer and longing at Jerusalem. Paul Chesley

As a documentary photographer, Kashi spends much of the year on the road working on topics of concern to him. In past essays, he has dealt with the heroin problem in Poland, culture and nightlife in Berlin, the return of the Soviet veterans from the Afghanistan war, and life in Eastern Europe. His latest personal project took him to Cairo to explore the City of the Dead, which was published in *Audubon* magazine and the *Observer Magazine* in London.

Nick Kelsh

American/Philadelphia, Pennsylvania
A native of North Dakota, Kelsh has produced award-winning photos for *Time, Life, Newsweek, National Geographic, Forbes, Fortune,* and *Business Week.* In 1986, he left the *Philadelphia Inquirer* to cofound Kelsh Wilson Design, a company that specializes in design and photography for annual reports and other corporate publications. Kelsh pictures are featured in *Boyz II Men: Us II You* and on the covers of *A Day in the Life of China, A Day in the Life of Thailand, America: Then & Now,* and *The Jews in America.*

Antonin Kratochvil

Czechoslovakian/New York
Born in Czechoslovakia in 1947, Kratochvil has been working in the United States as a freelance photographer since 1972. He continues to travel the world on assignment for *Discover , Newsweek,* the *New York Times,* the *Los Angeles Times, Smithsonian,* and *Condé Nast Traveler.* His work has appeared in numerous books, and he was named 1991 Photojournalist of the Year by the International Center of Photography. In 1992, he won a silver medal from the Art Directors Club of New York.

Miki Kratsman

Israeli/Tel Aviv
Born in 1959 in Buenos Aires, Argentina, Miki Kratsman moved to Israel in 1971. From 1987 until the present, he has been a photographer for the daily newspaper *Hadashot* and the Spanish publications *Cambio 16* and *Diario 16.* From 1991 until 1992, Kratsman was a teacher at Ramat Gan School of Art. He founded and managed the photo lab at *Hadashot* and served as a medical photographer at the Sourasky Medical Center in Tel Aviv. Kratsman has been honored with several exhibits of his work. He contributes to *Newsweek, Time,* and the French *Liberation.*

Hiroji Kubota

Japanese/Tokyo
Born in 1939 in Tokyo, Kubota graduated with a bachelor of arts in political science from Waseda University, Tokyo, in 1962. He lived

in New York and Chicago from 1962 until 1967 and became a freelance photographer in New York in 1965. Kubota has been a member of the renowned Magnum photo agency since 1971. His work has been published and exhibited worldwide and has been included in many books. His many awards include the prestigious Mainichi Art Award.

Daniel Lainé
French/Paris
Lainé started his career as a freelance photographer for *Liberation* and has worked for *Partir* and *Grand Reportages*, completing numerous travel stories in South America and Africa. Lainé has been a correspondent in Western and Central Africa for Agence France Presse and a staff photographer for *Actuel.* Lainé's pictures have been featured in *A Day in the Life of America, A Day in the Life of Spain,* and *The Circle of Life.* His own books include *Indios, Black Faces,* and *Kings of Africa.*

Vera Lentz
Peruvian/Lima
Vera Lentz was born in Peru and has lived in Europe and the United States. She freelances for major American and international publications. At present she is completing a book on Peru for W. W. Norton. She is associated with the Black Star Photo Agency in New York.

Gerd Ludwig
German/Los Angeles, California
A founding member of the Visum photo agency in Hamburg, Ludwig is a regular contributor to *GEO, Life, Stern, Fortune, Time,* and *Newsweek.*

He became a *National Geographic* contract photographer in 1992. Since then, he has worked on issue-driven subjects such as *The Broken Empire,* a lengthy report about changes in the former Soviet Union. Ludwig is also a veteran of numerous *Day in the Life* projects.

Pascal Maitre
French/Paris
Maitre has photographed conflicts the world over and has published his work in *GEO, Stern, Time, Life,* and *Le Figaro.* He has published three books: *Rwanda* (1991), *Barcelona* (1989), and *Zaire* (1985). In 1986, Maitre won a World Press Photo award for his work in Iran. He is associated with the agency GLMR Associés/SAGA Images.

James Marshall
American/New York
Cofounder of Pacific Rim Concepts, Marshall produced and edited *Hong Kong: Here Be Dragons,* published to critical praise in 1992. For the past fifteen years he has traveled

extensively in Europe and Asia, contributing work to international publications including *Newsweek,* the *New York Times, Smithsonian, Travel & Leisure,* and *U.S. News and World Report.* In 1987, he organized *Document: Brooklyn,* involving forty-five photographers recording one week in the life of this mythic American community, and thus became hooked on big productions. He is codirector of *A Day in the Life of Thailand* and *Planet Vegas.*

Susan Meiselas
American/New York
Susan Meiselas received her masters in education from Harvard University and her undergraduate degree from Sarah Lawrence College.

Her first major photographic essay, spanning several years, focused on the lives of carnival strippers in New England. She joined Magnum Photos in 1976. Meiselas's coverage of hostilities in Central America was published worldwide by the *New York Times Magazine,* the *London Sunday Times,*

Time, GEO, Paris Match, and *Machete,* among others. She won the Robert Capa Gold Medal from the Overseas Press Club in 1979 for her work in Nicaragua. Her two books are *Carnival Strippers* (1976) and *Nicaragua* (1981). Meiselas was an editor and contributor to the book *El Salvador: The Work of Thirty Photographers* and editor of *Chile from Within.*

Recently, Meiselas has been researching and photographing *In the Shadow of History: Kurdistan* for Random House. She has codirected two films: *Living at Risk: The Story of a Nicaraguan Family* (1986) and *Pictures from a Revolution* (1991). Meiselas has also received the Leica Award for Excellence and the Photojournalist of the Year Award from the American Society of Magazine Photographers. In 1992, Meiselas was named a MacArthur Fellow. She received a Photographer's Fellowship from the National Endowment of the Arts in 1984 and was awarded an honorary degree in Fine Arts from Parsons School of Design in 1986.

Ranks of chairs are readied for a Jerusalem Day reception for Mayor Ehud Olmert in Safra Square, near City Hall. Micha Bar'Am

Claus C. Meyer

German/Rio de Janeiro

The winner of many prizes and awards, Meyer was selected in 1985 by *Communications World* as one of the top annual-report photographers in the world. His excellence in color photography has been recognized by Kodak and Nikon, and in 1981 he won a Nikon International Grand Prize. He has published several books on Brazil, most recently a book on the Amazon in 1993.

Sylvia Plachy

American/New York

Sylvia Plachy's photographs have appeared in many publications. Her own book, *Unguided Tour,* won the Infinity Award from the International Center of Photography in 1990. Her most recent exhibit, *The Call of the Street,* was shown at the Whitney Museum at Philip Morris in 1993. Her photographs are in the collection of the Museum of Modern Art and the Metropolitan Museum in New York. She is currently working on books about Eastern Europe and about "red light" districts in the United States.

Larry Price

American/Fort Worth, Texas

A native Texan, Price began his photographic career at the *El Paso Times.* Later, he worked for the *Fort Worth Star-Telegram,* where he won a Pulitzer Prize for his coverage of the 1980 Liberian coup. His photographs from El Salvador and Angola for the *Philadelphia Inquirer* won him a second Pulitzer in 1985. His work has been honored by the Overseas Press Club, the National Press Photographers Association, the Associated Press, and the World

Press competition. Price is a seasoned contributor to the *Day in the Life* series.

Eldad Rafaeli

Israeli/Tel Aviv

Rafaeli studied at the Camera Obscura School of Art and Tel Aviv University. He has photographed for *Tel Aviv* and *Seven Days* newspapers. His many exhibitions include shows at the Camera Obscura Gallery and the Tel Aviv Museum.

Raghu Rai

Indian/New Delhi

Rai was born in December 1942. He qualified as civil engineer, but he started taking photographs at the age of twenty-four. Rai's photographs first appeared in the *Times of London* in the late 1960s. His major photo essays have appeared in various magazines and newspapers around the world, including *National Geographic, GEO, Life, Stern, Time,* and the *New York Times.* Rai has been on the jury of World Press Photo competition in Holland for two years. He has published eight marvelous books on different themes in India and has been a member of Magnum Photos since 1977.

Alon Reininger

American/Israeli/Los Angeles

Following a stint as a commercial photographer and assistant cameraman in Israel, Reininger turned to photojournalism in 1973 during the October War, which he covered for UPI. Since then, he has traveled extensively, documenting political and social change throughout the world. His work has appeared in *Time, Life,* the *New York Times Magazine,* and the *London Sunday Times.* Reininger's coverage

of the AIDS crisis has earned him awards from the National Press Photographers Association, the World Press Photo Foundation, and the American Society of Magazine Photographers. He is a founding member of Contact Press Images.

Rick Rickman

American/Laguna Nigel, California

Rick Rickman has been working as a photographer for seventeen years. During those years he has been assigned major stories all over the world. He contributes regularly to *Time* and *National Geographic* magazines. In 1985, he was presented the Pulitzer Prize for Spot News Photography. Some of his favorite assignments have been with past *Day in the Life* projects.

Razi (Richard) Robinowitz

Israeli/American/Tel Aviv

Born in New York, Razi immigrated to Israel in 1987, where he has spent the past seven years photographing for the weekend magazine sections of *Yediot Aharonoth,* Israel's largest-circulation daily. His work has also appeared in the *Jerusalem Post.* His own projects have taken him to Egypt, Turkey, Poland, and Brazil.

Steve Rubin

American/Baltimore, Maryland

Rubin's work is influenced by the documentary tradition of the 1930s and by his academic training in sociology. Undergraduate fieldwork among Gypsies led him to documentary photography, where he felt the concerns of sociology could be communicated visually. He has photographed the plight of Kurdish refugees, the destruction of the Ecuadorian rain forest, political turmoil in Pakistan, and

the transition to democracy in Chile. Closer to home, he has covered stories that include illegal immigration, the health-care crisis, and the not-so-romantic life of hoboes. He is currently an Alicia Patterson Foundation Fellow, completing a long-term photo essay, *Poverty in Vacationland: Life in a Backwoods Maine Community.* He has been honored with the Leica Medal of Excellence, a New York Foundation for the Arts Photography Fellowship, and an Award of Excellence from the National Press Photographers competition. He was a finalist for the W. Eugene Smith Award in Humanistic Photography in 1992 and 1993. His work has been published in the *New York Times Magazine,* the *Independent Magazine, Stern, GEO, L'Express, Time, Newsweek,* the *Village Voice,* and *Outtakes,* among others. He is represented by JB Pictures, New York.

David Rubinger

Israeli/Jerusalem

David Rubinger, perhaps Israel's most respected photographer, was born in Vienna in 1924 and came to Israel—then Palestine—in 1939 with Youth Aliyah. He spent the first years on a kibbutz and, at the age of eighteen, joined the British army during World War II. It was in service with the Jewish Brigade in Europe that he became interested in taking pictures. Returning to civilian life, he settled his family in Jerusalem and determined to turn what was a hobby into his life's work. Freelancing for several years, he was invited in 1951 to join *Ha'Olam-Hazeh* magazine, covering the Kastner-Grunwald trial. Since then, he has covered nearly every history-making event in the Middle East for *Time* and *Life.*

A Talmud teacher in the Hungarian Quarter of Mea Shearim. Emmanuel Santos

Shabtai Tal
Israeli/Tel Aviv
Born in Israel in 1939, Tal graduated from Betzalel Academy of Art in Jerusalem. He has been a press photographer since 1961. Highlights of his coverage include the Six-Day War in 1967 for *Time* and *Life,* the Yom Kippur War and the Israel-Egypt peace process (in Israel, Egypt, and Washington), the Intifada, the war in Lebanon (1982), and the Gulf War for *Stern.* Until 1991, Tal was bureau chief for *Stern* magazine in Israel. Today, Tal is a freelance photographer and correspondent for various German magazines. His exhibition *Man at War* was shown at the Jewish Museum in New York in 1974. His most famous photograph is a portrait of Israel's first prime minister, David Ben Gurion, which was printed in a widely circulated poster format.

Hana Sahar
Israeli/Ramat Gan
Hana Sahar currently works as a magazine photographer in Israel. She has been represented in several exhibitions in Israel and received a scholarship from the French government.

Jeffery Allan Salter
American/Miami, Florida
In high school, all his classmates called him "the cameraman." Now they know him as Jeffery Allan Salter, the award-winning photojournalist who has covered such global events as the bombing of the Pan Am airliner over Lockerbie, Scotland, and the deadly Haitian elections of November 1987. Currently, Salter is a staff photographer with the *Miami Herald.* Previously, he worked for *Newsday,* the *Bergen Record,* the *Virginian Pilot/ Ledger Star,* and *Navy Times.* Among

his many awards: Leica Medal of Excellence Finalist, Atlanta Seminar on Photojournalism, Photographer of the Year, New Jersey Photographer of the Year, American Photographer's New Face in Photojournalism Finalist, numerous first-place awards from the New York Press Photographers Association, and an Excellence in Photojournalism award from Sigma Delta Chi. His work has been included in recent books such as *The African Americans, A Day in the Life of Israel,* and *Songs of My People.*

Emmanuel Santos
Australian/Melbourne
A Filipino immigrant in Australia since 1982, Santos has produced photo essays and exhibitions on the human experience in China, Japan, India, the Philippines, Poland, and Australia. His work has appeared in both Australian

and worldwide publications. He has been working for a decade on a project on the lost tribes of Israel. He is a contributing photographer for Gamma Presse Images in Paris and a founding director of the M-33 Photo Agency in Melbourne.

Joel Sartore
American/Lincoln, Nebraska
Sartore began his photography career as a photo intern with the *Wichita Eagle* in 1984, becoming its director of photography in 1990. He has been a contract photographer with *National Geographic* magazine since 1992. Among his honors are the Award of Excellence, Magazine Photographer of the Year category in the 1992 Pictures of the Year competition, and 1986 Photographer of the Year, National Press Photographers Association, Region 7.

Scott Thode
American/New York
Scott Thode is a dedicated photographer whose work has appeared in *Life, Newsweek,* the *Independent, GEO, Il Venerdi,* and many other North American and European publications. His work has been exhibited at the Visa Pour L'Image photo festival in Perpignon, France, in the Electric Blanket AIDS Project, and at the P.S. 122 Gallery in New York City. In 1992, Thode was a finalist for the W. Eugene Smith Memorial Grant in Humanistic Photography. He won a first place at the Pictures of the Year competition sponsored by the National Press Photographers Association and took second place at the Gordon Parks Commemorative Photography Competition. Scott lives in New York City with his wife, Kathy Ryan, and their dog, Buster.

Nik Wheeler

British/Los Angeles, California

Nik Wheeler was born in Hitchin, England. He studied French and drama at Bristol University and French civilization at the Sorbonne, Paris. Wheeler's world travels began in Athens, where he taught English. His photographic career began in Bangkok, where he copublished a guide book to Thailand. In 1967, Wheeler moved to Vietnam as a combat photographer and joined United Press International during the 1968 Tet Offensive. In 1970, he went to the Middle East and covered the Jordanian Civil War for *Time,* the October War for *Newsweek,* and did assignments for *National Geographic* and *Paris Match.* In 1974, he moved to Paris and covered such diverse international events as the fall of Saigon, the Montreal Olympics, the U.S. presidential elections, and the coronation of the King of Nepal. Since 1977, he has been living in Los Angeles doing assignments for *National Geographic, GEO, International Wildlife,* and travel magazines such as *Travel and Leisure, Travel Holiday, Islands,* and *Departures.*

Wheeler's books include *Return to the Marshes* (1977), *Iraq—Land of Two Rivers* (1980), *This Is China* (1981), and *Cloud Dwellers of the Himalayas* (1982). Since 1986, he has been copublisher and principal photographer for the *Insider's Guides.* In addition to photography, he has written articles and columns for *Travel and Leisure, Islands,* and *Aramco World.* In 1988, he was named Photographer of the Year by the Society of American Travel Writers.

Marina Yurchenko

Russian/Moscow

After two years on the geography faculty of Moscow State University, Yurchenko decided to pursue a career in photojournalism. She has worked for *Sputnik* and the weekly *Moskovskiye Novosti* (*Moscow News*) and been a correspondent for the Novosti Press Agency since 1981. Yurchenko counts among her photographic specialties art, theater, and religion.

Memo Zack

Israeli/New York

Zack was born in Israel and lived there until he completed his military service. In 1962, Zack moved to New York City. After a sixteen-year career in the performing arts as a dancer and after completing a three-year program at City College of New York's Film Institute, he changed direction. With the encouragement and support of the renowned fashion photographer, Neal Barr, Zack decided to become a photographer. He spent five years as Barr's assistant and studio manager. In 1970, he left and opened his own studio specializing in fashion and beauty photography. During the past two years, Zack has spent half the year in New York City shooting for fashion and beauty clients and the other half traveling the world.

Sister Abraham (right), a Catholic nun from Denmark, resides with nuns of the Ethiopian Church, whom she instructs in foreign languages. **Jeffery Allan Salter**

FRIENDS AND ADVISORS

Bilal Abdul-Qader
Isaac Abraham
Ilan Adar
Herb Alexander
Ziva Almagor
Gali Amar
Shourouk As'ad
Nasser Attah
Irit Atzmon
Devorah Avidan
Yehuda Avner
Smadar Barber
Daniela Ben-Hefer
Brad Berman
Zadik Bino
Miri Bode
Arnon Bruckstein
Shoshana Cardin
Clayton Carlson
Drora Cass
Kathryn Chiba
Michael Claes
Hannah and Norman Cohen
Dan, Stacy, and Andrew Cohen
Dan Csasznik
Shoshannah Devorah
Anthea Disney
Kate Doty
Lois and Mark Eagleton
Mahmoud Abu Eid
Ruth and Robert Epstein
David Fatale
Maya Feller
Philip L. Fioresi
Seymour Fromer
Ken Fund
Anat Galili
Nelly and Nando Garcon
Salim Abu Gazala
Baruch Ghia
Baruch Gian
Meyrav Gilai
Michal Gotlib
Carolyn Greene
Marco Greenberg
Ardyn and Asnat Halter
Michal Heiman

Eliayahu Hendler
Sam Hoffman
Nicole Hohman
Michael Jankelowitz
Morris Joffe
Giovanna Judge
Anna Kamdar
Mira Kamdar
Pete Kamdar
Praveen and Caroline Kamdar
Yehuda Kaplan
Channa Kessler
Lu'ay Khoury
Robert Klein
Hilda Kline
Nitza Koerner
Keren and David Kremmerman
Mr. and Mrs. Stuart Lamb
Frances Lee
Tikvah Levine
Zvi Levran
Bori Liberman
Laini Liberman
The Liberman Family
Gene Lowenthal
Luay
Peter Macchia
Meirav Mack
Ariela Mader
Reda Mansour
Julie McCurry
Jeffrey Meltzer
Sandy Miller
Ida Mintz
Scott Montgomery
Genevieve Morgan
Nechama Moussaeff
Omer Naor
Hani Nasser-Edin
Reuven Nevo
Ehud Olmert
Allan Pakes
Gidon Patt
Kirsten Stoffregen Pedersen
Merav Peri
Aviva and Ilan Pivko
Deena Porat

Meir Porush
Nurit Pressman
John Pruzanski
Jarrad, Alexandra, and Leighton
  Pyke
Leah Rabin
Leon Recanati
Shula Recanati
Dr. Leslie Reti
Shmulik Reznik
Yitzhak Rogow
Daphna Rosenberg
Daniel Rossing
Natan Rotenberg
Russell Sacks
Bana Sa'eh
Joanna Samuels
Adi Semel
Yehuda Shafir
Tali Shchori
Shimon Sheinberger
Abraham Silver
Amiram Sivan
Jan Sloan
Jan Sommerville

Gadit Songo
Ytzhak Stein
Ian Stern
Dedier Stroz
Yossi Tal-Gan
Bernadette Toomey
David Tropper
Alona Vardi
Avi Varsano
Motti Verses
Doron Victor
Sarit Vidavsky
Samara Wacks
Colin Wade
Keri Walker
Barbara Weis
Nachum Yardeni
Shilo Yemini
Chaim Zucker

Special thanks to:
Zvi Raviv
International Coordinator,
Jerusalem 3000 Committee

ORGANIZATIONS

Academy Travel Ltd.
Africa Israel Hotels & Resorts Ltd.
Apple Center Tel Aviv/Europe House
Apple Computer, Inc.
Archaeological Seminars, Ltd.
Association of Israeli Insurance Companies
Association for Promoting Tourism in Israel
Bank Hapoalim
Ben Gurion Airport Security
Business Center, Hilton Hotel
BWC Imaging Labs
Camera Obscura School of Art
CLAL (Israel) Ltd.
Consulate General of Israel
Delek, The Israel Fuel Corporation Ltd.
Delta Film Ltd.
Eastman Kodak Company
El Al Israel Airlines Ltd.
Federation of Israeli Chambers of Commerce
Gitam/BBDO
Haskin Press
Hi Fi Lab
Hilton Hotel Tel Aviv
Holiday Inn Crowne Plaza, Jerusalem
IDF Spokesman
InnerAsia Expeditions
International Management Group

Iscar
Israel Discount Bank
Israel Insurance Association
Israel Ministry of Tourism
JDC Israel
Jerusalem Media & Communication Center
Keren Restaurant
Kesher Rent a Car Ltd./Hertz Licensee
Kinko's
Kodak AG Stuttgart
Light Waves
Luftansa German Airlines
Marina Super
Media Vault
Mivan Overseas Ltd.
Modern Effects
Moriah Hotels, Ltd.
New Lab
Office of the Mayor of Tel Aviv-Jaffa
Paz Oil Company Ltd.
Pelled Advertising & Promotion Ltd.
Sahar Investments
Shmiel Catering
Society for the Protection of Nature in Israel (SPNI)
Tel Aviv Hilton
TWA Airlines

BIBLIOGRAPHY

Ajami, Fouad. "Rediscovering Jerusalem." *U.S. News & World Report* 114, no. 9 (March 8, 1993): 74–81.

Alcalay, Ammiel. "The Geography of Time." *Michigan Quarterly Review* 31, no. 4 (fall, 1992): 498–515.

Alpert, Fran. *Getting Jerusalem Together*. Jerusalem: Archaeological Seminars, Inc., and Gefen Ltd., 1984.

Amichai, Yehuda. *Poems of Jerusalem and Love Poems*. New York: The Sheep Meadow Press, 1992.

Atkins, Norman. *Jerusalem*. APA Publications (HK) Ltd., 1988.

Back, Aaron. "The New Jerusalem." *Harper's Magazine* 282, no. 1690 (March 1991): 32–34.

Bahat, Dan. *Carta's Historical Atlas of Jerusalem*. Jerusalem: Carta, 1992.

———. "The Crusaders." *Les Dossiers d'Archéologie* (March 1992): 88–99.

Bellow, Saul. *To Jerusalem and Back*. New York: Viking Press, 1976.

Casson, Lionel. *Travel in the Ancient World*. Baltimore: Johns Hopkins University Press, 1994.

Coleman, Simon, and John Elsner. *Pilgrimage: Past and Present in the World Religions*. Cambridge, MA: Harvard University Press, 1995.

Collins, Larry, and Dominique Lapierre. *O Jerusalem!* New York: Simon & Schuster, 1988.

"Crazy? Hey, you never know." *Time* 145, no. 16 (April 17, 1995): 22.

Elon, Amos. *Jerusalem: City of Mirrors*. London: HarperCollins Publishers, 1991.

———. "Jerusalem: The Future of the Past." *New York Review of Books* 36, no. 13 (August 17, 1989): 37–39.

———. "Letter from Jerusalem." *New Yorker* 66, no. 10 (April 23, 1990): 92–101.

Gilbert, Martin. "A Tale of One City." *New Republic* 211, no. 20 (November 14, 1994): 17–24.

———. *Jerusalem: Rebirth of a City*. New York: Viking, 1985.

Goldberger, Paul. "Passions Set in Stone." *New York Times Magazine* (September 10, 1995): 42–77.

Gorenberg, Gershom. "Gone Shopping: Jerusalem Postcard." *New Republic* 211, no. 16 (October 17, 1994): 18–21.

Greenwood, Naftali, ed. *Israel Yearbook and Almanac 1994*. Jerusalem: Israel Business, Research, and Technical Translation/Documentation Ltd., 1994.

Har-El, Menashe. *This Is Jerusalem*. Jerusalem: Publishing House Kiryat-Sefer, Ltd., 1988.

Heschel, Abraham Joshua. *I Asked for Wonder*. New York: Crossroad, 1986.

Himelstein, Rabbi Dr. Shmuel. *The Jewish Primer*. Jerusalem: The Jerusalem Publishing House, Ltd., 1990.

Hovav, Gil. "The Road from Jerusalem." *Politika* (November 1988): 30–31.

Idinopulos, Thomas A. *Jerusalem*. Chicago: Elephant Paperbacks, Ivan R. Dee, 1994.

"Jerusalem Development Authority: Converting Human Assets into Technological Power." *Scientific American* 268, no. 6 (June 1993): 11–13.

Jones, Terry, and Alan Ereira. *Crusades*. Great Britain: Facts on File, 1995.

Josephus, Flavius. *The Life and Works of Flavius Josephus*. New York: Holt, Rinehart, and Winston.

Kimmerling, Baruch, and Joel S. Migdal. *Palestinians: The Making of a People*. New York: The Free Press, 1993.

Laurent, Annie. "The Thrice-Holy City." *UNESCO Courier* (May 1995): 14–16.

Lee, Rebecca. "The Jerusalem Syndrome." *Atlantic Monthly* 275, no. 5 (May 1995): 24–38.

Landau, David. *Piety and Power: The World of Jewish Fundamentalism*. New York: Hill and Wang, 1993.

Lightning Out of Israel: The Six-Day War in the Middle East. US: The Associated Press, 1967.

Malouf, Amin. *The Crusades through Arab Eyes*. New York: Schocken Books, 1985.

Margalit, Avishai. "The Myth of Jerusalem." *New York Review of Books* 38, no. 21 (December 19, 1991): 61–66.

Melman, Yossi. *The New Israelis: An Intimate View of a Changing People*. New York: Farrar, Strauss & Giroux, 1993.

Murphy-O'Connor, Jerome. "Christians and Christian Churches in Jerusalem." *Les Dossiers d'Archéologie* (March 1992): 78–87.

Oz, Amos. *Under This Blazing Light*. Cambridge, England: Cambridge University Press, 1979.

On the face of the Church of the Visitation in Ein Kerem, built in 1956, a mosaic portrays the Virgin Mary's visit to her relative Elizabeth, the mother of John the Baptist. It was during Mary's stay at Elizabeth's home—said to have stood on the sanctuary's site—that the Angel Gabriel announced to the Virgin that she would become the mother of the infant Jesus. **Steve Rubin**

Patai, Raphael. *Gates to the Old City: A Book of Jewish Legends.* New York: Avon Books, 1980.

Peters, F. E. *Jerusalem.* Princeton, NJ: Princeton University Press, 1985.

Pogrebin, Letty Cottin. "Two Forevers and a Maybe." *Tikkun* 8, no. 6 (November–December 1993): 72–74.

Rabinovich, Abraham. *"Jerusalem Today." Les Dossiers d'Archéologie* (March 1992): 120–31.

Reich, Ronny. "The Return of the Exile." *Les Dossiers d'Archéologie* (March 1992): 46–55.

Ribalow, Reena. "English and American Artists in 19th Century Jerusalem." *Les Dossiers d'Archéologie* (March 1992): 112–19.

Ronnen, Meir. "Teddy Kollek: A Vision of Parks and Gardens." *ARTnews* 94, no. 4 (April 1995): 101–3.

Rosen-Ayalon, Myriam. "Islamic Art and Architecture in Jerusalem." *Les Dossiers d'Archéologie* (March 1992): 100–111.

Slaughter, Frank G. *David: Warrior and King.* New York: Pocket Books, Inc., 1963.

Spencer, Diane. "Living Their Lives Against All the Odds." *Times Educational Supplement* 3980 (October 9, 1992): 12.

Stanger, Theodore, and Eetta Prince-Gibson. "Settlers Inside the Walls: Remaking the Muslim Sector of Ancient Jerusalem." *Newsweek* 119, no. 6 (February 10, 1992): 36.

Surkes, Sue. "Victims of the Peace Settlement." *Times Educational Supplement* 4113 (April 28, 1995): 16.

"This Year in Jerusalem." *The New Republic* 212, no. 23 (June 5, 1995): 9–10.

Thubron, Colin. *Jerusalem.* Boston: Little, Brown & Company, 1969.

Tsafrir, Yoram. "Jerusalem in the Roman and Byzantine Periods." *Les Dossiers d'Archéologie* (March 1992): 66–77.

Wagner, Donald E. "Holy Land Christians Worry about Survival." *Christian Century* 108, no. 14 (April 24, 1991): 452–53.

Wall, James M. "Shaping Reality: A Visit to Jerusalem." *The Christian Century* 111, no. 35 (December 7, 1994): 1147–48.

Werblowsky, R. J. Zwi. "Jerusalem, Holy City." *Les Dossiers d'Archéologie* (March 1992): 6–13.

Illustration credits pages 4–13:

Pages 4, 6–8, 10, and 11, Archive Photos; pages 5 and 9 from *The Family Bible* printed by A. J. Holman & Co., 1882.

Quiet archways shade the
Jewish Quarter of the Old City.

Ed Kashi